How To Raise, Train and Compete

Frisbee®Dogs

By Peter Bloeme, World Frisbee Champion

PRB & Associates • Atlanta, Georgia

Design by Cohen & Company, Atlanta, Georgia. Cover photograph of Wizard by Jackie Bernard. Title page photograph of Peter Bloeme and Wizard by Tom Nebbia. Final editing done by Janet Cotter.

Every effort has been made to trace the copyright holders and models of the photographs used in this book. Should there be any omissions in this respect, the publisher apologizes and shall be pleased to make the appropriate acknowledgements in any future printings.

FRISBEE is a registered trademark of Wham-O, Inc., U.S. Trademark Reg. No. 679,186, issued May 26, 1959, for toy flying saucers for toss games. The term "Frisbee," as used in the title and text of this book, refers solely to the flying discs manufactured and sold by Wham-O, Inc. under the trademark Frisbee®. The first letter of the word Frisbee is capitalized throughout this book as the method chosen to signify that the term is a registered trademark. No use of the word Frisbee in this book should be assumed to imply that Frisbee is a game or sport rather than a toy flying disc.

ISBN 0-9629346-0-7

First Edition/First Printing August 1991

Library of Congress Catalog Number: 91-90260

Copyright © 1991 by PRB & Associates. All rights reserved including the right of reproduction in whole or in part in any form.

Printed in the United States of America.

The Far Side cartoon by Gary Larson *(see page 36)* is reprinted by permission of Chronicle Features, San Francisco, CA.

To order additional copies of this book, contact the publisher:
> **PRB & Associates**
> *4060–D Peachtree Road, Suite 326*
> *Atlanta, Georgia 30319*
> *(404) 231-9240*

Production Notes
This book was produced entirely on the desktop with Macintosh computers using DesignStudio. Roughs were printed on a LaserWriter IINT. Cover photos were scanned on a ColorGetter and separated on an AGFA SelectSet 5000. Black and white photos were scanned on an AGFA Focus II S800 GSE Scanner and retouched with ColorStudio. Film was run on the AGFA StudioSet 2000 Imagesetter.

Contents

1   **Introduction**

5   **History Of The Frisbee**

9   **Canine Frisbee History**

15   **Peter Bloeme/Whirlin' Wizard**

27   **Key Canine Considerations**
Selecting A Dog • Health • Teeth • Nutrition • Naming Your Dog • Grooming • Nails • Obedience • Commands • Basic Training Techniques • Common Injuries • Discipline

41   **Frisbee Basics**
Disc Selection • Gimmicks • Gumabone Frisbee Flexible Flying Disc • Frisbee Care And Maintenance • Frisbee Aerodynamics

51   **Throwing**
Grip • Spin • Stance • General Elements • Backhand • Roller • Upside-Down Slider • Upside-Down • Advanced Throws • Skip • Sidearm • Two-Handed • Non-Standard Throws

63   **Basic Frisbee Training**
Workout Area • Weather Conditions • Frisbee Familiarization • Tracking • Frisbee Basics • Warm-Ups • Catching • Jumping

73   **Advanced Frisbee Training**
"Over" • "Take" • "Give"/"Drop" • Vaulting • Multiples • Front Flip And Back Flip • Tapping/Tipping • Multiple Disc Catches • Butterfly • Props

87   **Competition**
Competitive Events • Basic Throw And Catch • Mini-distance • Freeflight • Degree Of Difficulty • Execution • Leaping Agility • Showmanship • Local Competition • Regional And World Finals • World Champions • Hall Of Fame • Contest Promotion

97   **Competition Tips**
Know The Rules • Be Creative • Practice All The Events • Choreography • Appearance/Costumes • Strategy • Working With The Media, Sponsor, Competition, Exhibition, General

101   **Travel**
Kennels And Crates • Air Travel • The Flight Explained • Food And Water • Hotels

107   **Collecting Discs**

111   **Wizard's Competitive Experience**

117   **Professional Appearances**

129   **Afterword**

131   **Appendix**

133   **Index**

A neighborhood dog dives in a San Francisco fountain to keep cool.

This book would not have been possible without the people and organizations listed below. Some contributed more than others but everyone's help was greatly appreciated.

AGFA Compugraphic, Michael Anderson, Chris Barbo, Jackie Bernard, Reese Blake, Jack Bornstein, Allyn Rice Bloeme, Erik Borg, Tad Bowen, Esther Branch, Chris Breit, Craig Brownell, Abby Burton, Jeff Carlick, Peter Carlos, Chronicle Features, Forest Clayton, Barbara Cohen, Cohen & Company, Come 'N Get It Dog Food, Karl Cook, Janet Cotter, Bob Cox, Delta Air Lines, John Disney, Barbara Dugan, Charles Duran, Joanne Duran, Robin Duran, Ron Ellis, Tony Frediani, Lynne Frye, Jeff Gabel, John Gentry, Gary Gomes, Rick Guebert, Terri Hanson, Jeff Hartshorne, Florence Hill, Richard Hill, Mary Hall, Bernie Holmes, Jendi Holmes, Spencer Huender, Tia Joslin D.V.M., Henry Khoo, Karen Knox, Robert Knox, Irv Lander, Gary Larson, Bethe Lehman, Letraset, David Letterman, Long Photography, Inc., Brenda Maceo, Walt Mancini, Pete McCabe, Lou McCammon, Eldon McIntire, Glenn Medford, Kathy Miller, Mike Miller, Betty Moore, Cynthia Mullennix, Bill Murphy, National Enquirer, Tom Nebbia, Jackie Nickerson, Glenn Osaki, Robert Ozankan, Cheryl Padgett, Greg Perry, Jeff Perry, Sas Peters, Ken Pogson, Glenn Provenzano, Janis Rettaliata, David Robinson, Dan Roddick, Manny Rodriguez, Job Sargent, Larry Schindel, Donna Schoech, Stan Sellers, Mike Smith, Alex Stein, Gary Suzuki, Larry Taylor, Phil Van Tee, Time Magazine, Robin Wade, Don Wakefield, Bill Watters, Ashley Whippet, Whirlin' Wizard, Tom Wehrli, Valdo Williams, Wolf Camera, Mark Wood, Miles Wright, and my wife Lynn Duran

"Catch that for me, won't you Chauncy?"

PHIL VAN TEE

1989 World Champion Gilbert in Berlin, Germany, August 1990

Foreword

It's very entertaining to see dogs soaring through the air to catch flying discs, but Frisbee dogs don't just miraculously develop overnight. Training even the most adaptable breeds, like Australian Shepherds, Labrador Retrievers and Border Collies, requires dedication and patience to achieve gratifying results.

When my friend Peter Bloeme asked me to write a foreword for this book, I was flattered. As co-founder and Executive Director of the Ashley Whippet Invitational, along with my 10 year stint as Vice President and member of the Board of Directors of the Los Angeles Society for the Prevention of Cruelty to Animals I have seen many newspaper articles and books written about Frisbee and dog training. Many writers, in an attempt to be cute or funny, have not taken the subject seriously. Peter has worked long and hard to achieve personal success and professional stature by being a pioneer in the sport, a world champion, a professional performer, a national judge and a world-class dog trainer. He takes Frisbee seriously, which is why you'll find the material in this book authoritative and sincere.

In any event, I received the invitation to set the tone of this truly excellent and comprehensive work on the care and training of a Frisbee dog with much enthusiasm. I hope what I say measures up to Peter's expectations, because he sets high standards of perfection for himself and others.

Is the book timely? Does it fill a need? Emphatically, YES! The national interest in acquiring and training a dog to be adept at catching a Frisbee, is at an all-time high, thanks to the exploits of high-flying canines on television and in the print media.

Individuals who now own an untrained dog, or who plan to acquire one, will benefit

Cheryl Padgett's alert Aussies

greatly from this book. Peter shares with the reader his many experiences as a gifted athlete and the methods he used to train the undefeated 1984 World Champion Whirlin' Wizard, his beloved Border Collie. And Peter does it in a down-to-earth, narrative style that while factual and logical, makes for fascinating reading. While it may be true that every expert is not necessarily a good teacher, Peter is the real thing. He gives you practical step-by-step guidance, not theory, with his uncanny knack for making complex things seem simple.

Reading this book in manuscript form, I became even more aware of Peter's greatest asset: perseverance. Without perseverance in the pursuit of learning and excellence, one will not achieve success to the desired degree. The key is there for you in this book, but you must not be impatient or give up along the way.

Many people have told me they were inspired to get and train a Frisbee dog after seeing Peter perform with Wizard on television or in a stadium. Now they, and you, can intimately share his unique repertoire of tricks by owning this book and by reading and re-reading it thoroughly.

If you're serious about raising and training a Frisbee dog, and becoming a skilled thrower as well, this book by Peter Bloeme is a "must." Like Peter, it is World Class in every respect.

Irv Lander
Executive Director, Come 'N Get It Canine Frisbee disc Championships

Peter Bloeme, Alex Stein and Irv Lander with Wizard, Ashley Whippet III and II.

Introduction

Why teach your dog to play Frisbee? There are many reasons:

One: It's a fantastic way to keep a dog in excellent condition by promoting cardiovascular development. The running and jumping involved in the sport improves muscular strength and prevents misdirected energy.

Two: Frisbee is great for a dog's eyesight! While both improving and strengthening vision, it helps him track (follow) and focus on a small moving object.

Three: It promotes camaraderie between owner and pet and creates a special bond of friendship. It gives the dog a special reason for living.

Four: Playing with a Frisbee and teaching your dog to play is a challenge for both of you. It offers an opportunity for you to share an interest as a team. And, if you decide to compete, it can involve the whole family.

Five: Frisbee competitions are open to all dogs regardless of breeding and size. Pound puppies can compete "paw-to-paw" with purebred canines. Because of this, many dogs have been rescued from the pound, and almost certain death, because the adopter found a dog that would make a good companion and playmate.

Six: There can be many positive intangibles due to your participation in the sport. I met my wife Lynn, when, as a television producer, she interviewed me while I was performing with Wizard. Because of Frisbee you might make a life-long friend, appear on television, or compete at the world championships.

1984 World Champions, Whirlin' Wizard and Peter Bloeme, with puppy Magic.

1989 World Champion, Gilbert, about to make a saving catch.

Still, the most basic reason for teaching your dog to play is simply that dogs LOVE IT!

You may not have a world champion on your hands, but if you read this book carefully and follow the instructions outlined, I'm sure that you will have your dog running, jumping and catching in no time, while providing endless moments of enjoyment for both of you.

How This Book Is Organized

The primary focus of this book is on training your dog to play Frisbee, yet, I am often asked how I became involved in Frisbee and what it was like to do various professional shows. Therefore, I have also included this personal information. I hope that by doing so, you will be entertained and perhaps learn something from my experiences. I have also chosen to write somewhat chronologically, in what I feel is a logical, step-by-step order.

Some Personal Thoughts

I found that once I began writing about Frisbee and dogs, I wanted to include so much material on raising and training a dog to a world class level that things quickly got out of hand. Therefore, to cover the topic in a unique, adaptable and useful manner, I concentrated on the areas that I felt to be the most valuable to the typical dog owner. I recommend that you combine the guidance in this book with the resources listed in the Appendix for the best results.

After beginning work on this manuscript, I realized I wanted another dog.

Introduction

My world champion dog, Whirlin' Wizard is, at the time of this writing, 8 years old and deserves to retire from the daily routine of performing. Having a puppy to train while writing a book on training a dog is certainly advantageous, so it was easy to justify to myself (and my wife) the addition of a new pup. I purchased an 11-week-old Australian Shepherd, whom I named Magic. He looked a lot like Wizard but without a long tail with which to sweep off the coffee table. The third day I had him we traveled to Dallas, Texas, where I appeared as a member of the Come 'N Get It Celebrity Team. While there, Magic made his first appearance on NBC television chasing a disc. So I see him in the future catching in Wizard's "pawsteps."

To eliminate possible confusion and to make writing easier, I will, for the most part, use male pronouns when I refer to all dogs unless I know they are female. Both my dogs are male, therefore it was more natural for me to use a masculine reference.

As you pursue this activity and work with your pet, please feel free to write me with your discoveries and insights. I welcome your comments and new ideas as the great sport of canine Frisbee play continues to grow, develop and evolve.

Write to: **Peter Bloeme**
PRB & Associates
4060-D Peachtree Road, Suite 326
Atlanta, Georgia 30319

Nine Poodle pups born to Frisbee-dog father Bentley, owned by Judy and J.P. Rees.

Don Wakefield and Carbo dazzle spectators at the LA County Fairgrounds.

History of the Frisbee

Most people who become involved with canine Frisbee are led to the sport by their dogs and are usually unaware of the early history of Frisbee play. Other people (like myself), enter the sport through disc sports. Either way, I feel that it is important to know the history of the disc.

In 1871, a man named William Russell Frisbie settled in Bridgeport, Connecticut and took over the management of a new bakery. Soon after, he bought it outright and renamed it "The Frisbie Pie Company." At its peak it turned out more than 80,000 pies per day!

Gay Talese of the *New York Times* wrote on August 11, 1957:

"Possibly the name is used in recognition of the Frisbie Baking Company of Bridgeport, Connecticut, which after World War II had a clientele notoriously famous for not returning tin pie plates.

"'Somebody discovered a pie-plate-pitching game and it was found that our tin plates were excellent for scaling (throwing),' a company official said. 'During that fad we lost about 5,000 tin pie plates.'"

Two weeks later, on August 25, 1957, the Times published the following letter:

"...It is common knowledge in New Haven that Frisbie has been played at Yale for over a century...at Yale, birthplace of the sport, Frisbie is a heritage—a whole way of life."

Credit for the development of the modern plastic product can be given to Walter Fred Morrison, whose father invented the sealed-beam auto headlight. In 1947 Morrison carved the first

Original Frisbee Pie Tin

flying disc from a block of tenite (an early plastic). He soon found that tenite was too brittle, so in 1948 he used a plastic that could be molded.

According to Dr. Stancil E.D. Johnson in his book, *Frisbee*, "*This original Morrison's Flyin' Saucer was his Arcuate Vane Model, named for the six topside (flight plate) curved spoilers (vanes)...Curiously, the spoilers were on backward; that is, they would theoretically work only for a counterclockwise spin.*" That disc was the predecessor of today's Frisbee discs.

In late 1955, Wham-O Manufacturing Company's (hereafter simply referred to as Wham-O) founders, Rich Knerr and A.K. "Spud" Melin (who started their company in a garage where they produced sling shots), saw the "Pluto Platter" (Morrison's revised "Arcuate Vane") and liked the product so much that they purchased the rights to manufacture and sell it.

On January 13, 1957 the first Pluto Platter rolled off the Wham-O production line; in 1958 the Frisbie Pie Company went out of business, signalling the end of one era and the beginning of another.

Dr. Johnson also wrote in his book *Frisbee:*

"*On a trip to the campuses of the Ivy League, Knerr first heard the term frisbie. Harvard students said they'd tossed pie tins around for years and called it frisbieing. Knerr liked the terms frisbie and frisbieing, so he borrowed them.*

Frisbee dog statue in Milford, Connecticut by Patrick Villers Farrow

Four-time World Finalists Mark Wood and Zach

Having no idea of the historical origins, he spelled the saucer Frisbee, phonetically correct, but one vowel away from the Frisbie Pie Company."

And in the May 1975 edition of *Oui Magazine,* James R. Petersen wrote:

"To avoid legal trouble with the Frisbie Pie Company, Fred Morrison changed the ie to ee and patented the Frisbee Flying Disk [sic]. It was a cosmic example of name it and claim it. Like Kleenex, like Xerox, Frisbee became the noun for all varieties of the product. Unlike Kleenex, like Xerox, Frisbee also became a verb and a way of life."

On May 26, 1959, Wham-O was granted a registered trademark on the word "Frisbee." It is trademark number 679,186 for "Toy flying saucers for toss games." Called everything from disc, to disk, to sport disc, to flying disc, to flying saucer, there has never been a more widely accepted name for this product than the original term Frisbee (Frisbee disc by Wham-O), which has been used now for more than 30 years.

The meaning behind the word Frisbee transcends the flying disc. It is, and has always been, a sport and a way of life. Since its first use as a pie tin, this "toy" became a fad, turned game, then sport, and took off in popularity. Frisbee has gained respectability; today it's taught and played in many schools and universities. There is now a World Flying Disc Federation based in Sweden with 26 member nations plus a number of contests, mail order businesses and publications devoted to this world class sport.

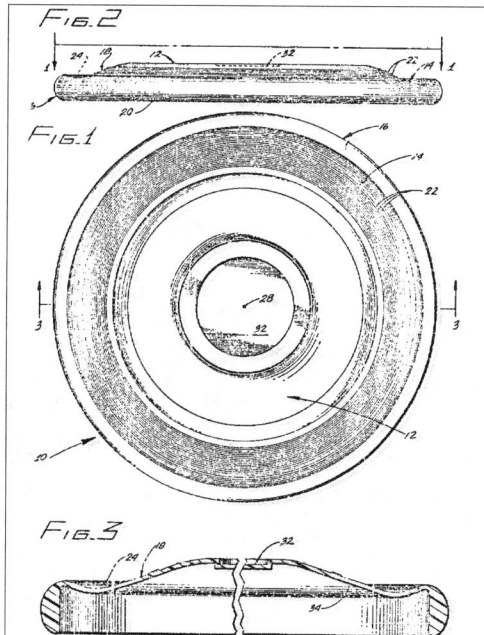

Figure at left is a Wham-O patent drawing of the Fastback Frisbee. This text is from the patent description.

"Over the past decade, toys resembling inverted platters or saucers have enjoyed great popularity as recreational items for use in throwing games and contests. In the usual embodiment the toy is made of a plastic material in a circular configuration with a rim portion located at its periphery, the rim portion being relatively thick in comparison to the remaining portions of the implement. In its normal inverted platter orientation, the rim curves downwardly from the toy body giving the implement a shape which approximates that of an airfoil when viewed in elevation. Such a toy has been marketed for the period indicated above by the assignee of the present application under the trademark Frisbee."

Three-time World Champion Ashley Whippet flies over Malibu Beach.

Canine Frisbee History

No one can actually pinpoint who was the first person to throw a Frisbee to his or her dog, but the credit for popularizing this activity must go to Alex Stein, owner and trainer of the legendary three-time world canine Frisbee champion, Ashley Whippet. Besides being his registered name, Ashley actually was a Whippet; a breed that looks like a small Greyhound—sleek, smooth, short-haired and very fast.

Ashley was born in Oxford, Ohio on October 2, 1971. Stein received him as a gift and took him everywhere. He soon discovered that he had no ordinary run-of-the-mill dog! Ashley would chase, leap gracefully, spin in the air and catch just about any disc thrown (which at the time were large Super Pro Frisbees).

Stein had the intuition that Ashley could make it in show business, so he boldly moved from Cleveland, Ohio to Hollywood, California; the land of opportunity for the unusual.

When he called the various talent agencies, he said he had a dog that ran 35 miles-per-hour, jumped nine feet, spun in the air and caught Frisbees. They answered, "You have a dog that can run how fast, jump how high and catch what?" then hung up. But Stein was not a quitter; he even approached Wham-O, the maker of Frisbee discs. At first, Wham-O showed no interest, so Stein dreamed up of a way to attract their attention. He had to prove that Ashley was attention-grabbing, exciting, newsworthy and entertaining. Fortunately, both Stein and Ashley had great courage, talent and determination.

Ashley Whippet Jr. jumps for joy in Berlin, Germany while Alex Stein looks on.

Alex Stein and Ashley Whippet entertained thousands at football game halftimes.

In August of 1974, Stein smuggled Ashley into Dodger Stadium during a nationally televised baseball game. Between the seventh and eighth innings, the duo ran onto the field and performed for eight minutes before Stein was arrested. Their debut almost turned catastrophic when, during the arrest, Ashley disappeared. Irv Lander, then Director of the International Frisbee Association, happened to be at the game and bailed Stein out of jail. For three days, both men were sick with worry at the thought that Ashley might be lost forever. Fortunately, a boy who had seen the performance found Ashley roaming the stadium parking lot. He had taken him home and cared for him until his parents could get in touch with Stein.

The crowd loved the impromptu show which brought the pair national publicity. Since that memorable baseball game, Stein and Ashley have become legendary among Frisbee aficionados, performing at Super Bowl XII, *"The Tonight Show," "Merv Griffin," "Late Night with David Letterman"* and even at the White House for Amy Carter. Then, when competition began for canines, Ashley ran away with three world titles.

Why Ashley was so talented no one knows. Whippets, in general, are not renowned Frisbee dogs. Still, I have never seen a dog more beautiful or as graceful, as fast or as high a leaper as Ashely.

After an action packed life of entertaining millions and popularizing an exciting activity for owners and their dogs, Ashley Whippet passed away on March 11, 1985 at the age of 14.

In his lifetime, Ashley set the standards for the sport. Yet he was just the beginning. People often ask me who is, or was, the greatest Frisbee dog. I can't compare Ashley or other great Frisbee dogs of the past with the champions of today because of the sport's rapid growth and development. New tricks, rules and training methods have all added variables that make comparisons difficult.

Another owner/dog team deserving credit for making the sport what it is today, is Eldon McIntire and his Australian Shepherd, Hyper Hank. They rank in the annals of canine Frisbee history, and few dogs are as aptly named. Hyper Hank perfectly complemented Ashley Whippet. Ashley was small, sleek and mellow; Hank was large and excitable. He would run through a wall to catch a disc, and dare I say hyper? McIntire and Hyper Hank frequently toured with Stein and Ashley. Their many historic canine Frisbee performances together included performances at the Super Bowl and at the White House.

Although the dogs themselves frequently get the accolades (and rightfully so!), we would not be where we are today without the incredible dedication, drive, energy and support from Irv Lander, who has always been a dog lover.

After seeing these great dogs perform, Lander felt that the opportunity existed to provide both a sponsor with an attention getting event and competitors with a unique and exciting competitive sport. A competition would serve many purposes. It would showcase trained dogs, encourage and provide a forum for up-and-coming dogs and give the human competitors an event to

Eldon McIntire and Hyper Hank were early innovators of the sport.

Ashley Whippet soars skyward as pal Hyper Hank watches in amazement.

Lady Ashley, daughter of Ashley Whippet, shows off her form.

Amy Carter throws to Ashley Whippet on the White House lawn in 1977 while Irv Lander (left), Alex Stein (second from right) and a friend watch.

work in partnership with their canine counterparts. Lander, who had worked closely for many years with the Society for the Prevention of Cruelty to Animals (SPCA) in Los Angeles, felt that an additional side benefit from the sport of canine Frisbee would be to encourage people to adopt pets from shelters.

In the beginning, Lander held the contest in conjunction with the World Frisbee Championships at the Rose Bowl. The support of a corporate sponsor allowed him to redesign the event so that it could stand on its own.

Lander made many sacrifices to keep the sport alive: he worked on a shoestring budget the first few years in order to establish the contest, he stayed in flea-bag motels while on the road, and also invested a great deal of his own money in order to ensure the success of the contest.

Lander's hard work and sacrifice resulted in a contest that today provides a sponsor with a wholesome promotional tie-in. The dogs make the contest a family-oriented media event, free to the public and a great time for all.

In honor of Lander's efforts, the members of the 1990 Canine Frisbee Celebrity Touring Team created the "Lander Cup." This new symbol for the sport is similar to hockey's "Stanley Cup" and lists all the world champions in the sport. It is displayed in the offices of the Ashley Whippet Invitational, which the contest is now named. *(See page 85 for more information on this event.)*

Hyper Hank tracks one down on the beach.

The three foot tall "Lander Cup" features the engraved names of all the World Champions and their dogs.

Three-time World Champion Alex Stein releasing Ashley Whippet Jr. for a distance throw.

Peter Bloeme/Whirlin' Wizard

The first two chapters of this book have set the stage with information on the history of the flying disc and the sport of canine Frisbee. My development in Frisbee ran a parallel path on the human side to Alex Stein and Ashley Whippet's.

I still remember the first day I threw a Frisbee. When I was twelve years old in 1968, my cousin Lynne and her boyfriend Moose took me to Central Park in New York City. While Lynne watched, Moose attempted to teach me how play Frisbee. As many people do at first, I threw it a long distance, but not in the direction I was aiming. Moose seemed frustrated by constantly having to run after my throws, but I was hooked, and Frisbee became my new challenge.

About a year later while walking through Central Park, my friend Job Sargent and I saw some people (who back then were called "hippies") playing Frisbee. We wanted to join in their game but were too shy to ask. We waited, hoping a wild throw would come our way and eventually, one did. I ran after it and threw it back. After this happened a few times, they asked us if we wanted to join them. Both Sargent and I did, and we went on to discover that people gathered at that spot every day to socialize and play Frisbee. From that point on, we went there every chance we had. It was not an area especially well suited for playing: the field was small—about 30 yards long and 40 yards wide, and because of a gradual slope on one end that dropped down to Central Park's rowboat lake, it was known as "Frisbee Hill."

The daily scene consisted of informal groups: "throwers," "middle-men," and "chasers." "Throwers" stayed at the top of the hill and threw Frisbees down to the "chasers," while the "middle men" threw to each other.

Peter Bloeme at 15 years of age.

World Champion Peter Bloeme at ages 15, 19 and 28 performing the same behind-the-back catch.

Whenever the two best throwers on the hill, Jim and Mel, challenged each other to a "hill throw" (a term used to describe how far they could throw the Frisbee), everything stopped. It was a beautiful sight, watching the discs gently curve over and then down the hill. As "chasers," Sargent and I would follow the discs, try to make catches and relay them back. I credit my unusual, but successful, long distance throwing style to being a "chaser." It took a different technique to throw up the hill, and as time passed, I could return those "hill throws" all the way from the bottom. Occasionally, for variety, we joined the "middle men" to work on trick throws and catches.

Since nearly everyone I played Frisbee with was older than I was, I didn't realize how good I was for my own age until I entered the Junior Frisbee Tournament in 1972. Designed for children 15 years old and under, it was hosted nationwide by local parks and recreation departments and was sponsored by Wham-O.

In my first distance event I threw a Frisbee 90 yards: not only did the throw surpass the 60-yard scoring maximum, but the Frisbee continued to fly over the recreation building at the end of the field, astonishing the officials.

I went on to win the city, state and then regional championships. As the East Coast Champion, I won free airline tickets for myself and an adult chaperon to the National Junior Frisbee Finals in Las Vegas, Nevada. I chose my coach and friend, Valdo Williams, a professional jazz pianist and karate expert, to accompany me. Williams, whom I met in the

Valdo Williams

park, became a father figure to me over the years, as my father passed on when I was 10. Williams and I spent much of our free time playing Frisbee together. The fact that he did not drink or use drugs made Williams a very positive influence on those around him.

I finished third overall at the Nationals and first in distance out of more than one and a half million junior competitors from all over the United States. It was there that I first met Irv Lander, then the National Junior Frisbee Contest Director. After the tournament, I wrote him a letter thanking him for running the contest in a professional and smooth manner. In return, I received an unexpected and memorable reply. He wrote:

"...*Although you did not achieve your goal this time, you were far and away the most spectacular Frisbee performer in the history of our National Junior Frisbee Championships.*

"*Surely there will be many additional honors that your skills and dedication will earn for you in the future. I am certain that your name will be prominent in adult Frisbee competition for years to come....*"

Since then, Lander has been a great influence on my personal and professional life, and working with him is always a pleasure and an honor. Lander, because of his love for Ashley and the sport of canine Frisbee, became the national director for the Ashley Whippet Invitational and is, as mentioned previously, primarily responsible for the organized sport as it exists today.

In 1975, I earned my World Class Masters rating (Frisbee's highest) by successfully completing the International Frisbee Association's proficiency test, which required many assorted throws and catches. It took place at the World Frisbee Championships (WFC) in the famed Rose Bowl in Pasadena, California.

In 1976 I practiced ardently for several hours every day. Early in the season at the Eastern National Championships, known as "Octad," I set a short lived world record in Throw, Run and Catch (TRC), an event that measures the distance a person runs between his throw and his catch (my TRC was 213 feet). More importantly, I won the Eastern National Overall title. Later that year, I went to Boston and won the Eastern National Distance title and came close to setting another world record.

Before the tournament, the world distance record was 366 feet. I finished with a throw of 375 feet! No one can say how much farther my throw would have gone had it not been stopped cold by a fence. Unfortunately, I was a day too late to set the world record, because on the previous day in the semi-finals, Dave Johnson, a tall, thin and very powerful man, made a throw of 412 feet!

By doing well at those two tournaments I earned another invitation to the World Frisbee Championships at the Rose Bowl. This was the beginning of a much tougher tournament format. To win the overall, one had to score well in six events. I competed against more than 100 of the top Frisbee players from around the world. All the front runners started strong, but after the second day the field narrowed, and by the third day it was a race between John Kirkland, a college professor from Boston, and myself, with accuracy as the deciding event.

Peter Bloeme demonstrating a difficult freestyle combination.

Kirkland approached me the evening before the accuracy event. He told me that he was going to beat me and win the overall title. I have to admit that I was a little intimidated because accuracy had always been my weakest event. I knew that he expected me to choke; instead, his boastful comments gave me the motivation I needed to really concentrate. That night, I planned my strategy, and since I wanted to remain focused, I cancelled my scheduled morning television appearance on the Mickey Mouse Show. I wanted to throw early in the day, when the weather was calm and I would have no distractions while Kirkland was shooting the show.

In the morning the weather was clear, allowing me to compete under ideal conditions for accuracy. When Kirkland arrived in the afternoon, he asked me how I had done. When I told him my score of 16 out of 28 (my best ever), I think it caused HIM to choke. Ironically, on the final day, I not only won the world

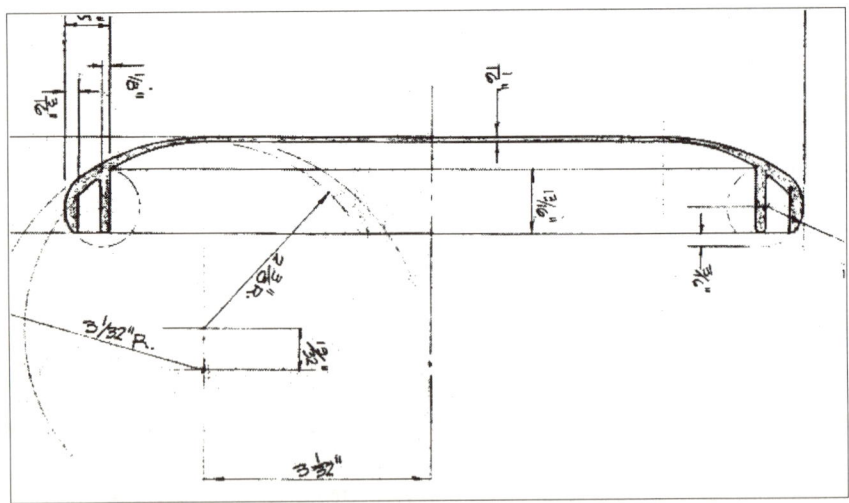

PETER BLOEME'S PATENT: *The theoretical advantage of this design over others is that there is more mass along the edge which should improve distance thrown. Additionally, the inner rim provides a better gripping surface which would allow greater control of throws.*

accuracy title but the Men's Overall World Frisbee Champion title as well. UPI (United Press International) wire service reported after the event:

"The contest was destined to be an anticlimax. After all, among the entrants in the World Frisbee Championships was John Kirkland, the Massachusetts Institute of Technology professor who specializes in the physics and aerodynamics of sustained Frisbee flight. He had honed his art to perfection because he found it 'spiritually fulfilling.'

"Once the air had cleared on championship day in Los Angeles, the academic emerged with a firm grip on the prize—for second place. Peter Bloeme, a 19-year-old New York City resident, apparently said nothing profound enough to be quoted. He finished first."

Because I had won two world titles, I was eligible for an endorsement contract with Wham-O, which I gratefully accepted. I considered it more of an honor than a financial jackpot. My name appeared on all their 1977 World Class Model Frisbee Discs.

It was at this championship that I first met and became friends with Alex Stein, the owner of Ashley Whippet. I also mingled with the other Frisbee dog owners who were there to compete in the canine world championships. The dogs' abilities astonished me, and although I loved dogs, I resented their popularity with the media and the public. As a human competitor, I sometimes felt ignored and jealous. The dogs appeared limited to jumping and catching, and it didn't seem fair that I spent hours each day practicing and perfecting technique and style only to receive less attention. Now, of course, because of my involvement in canine Frisbee, I feel differently.

The following year, I worked part-time as a Frisbee pro. Occasionally, I worked with Stein throwing long distance throws to Ashley Whippet, which led me to judging local canine Frisbee contests.

One of my most unusual competitive experiences took place at the Eastern Accuracy Championship in Tampa, Florida. Everything ran late the second day of this tournament and when we reached the finals of accuracy, it was dark. Some judges and competitors drove their cars with headlights on onto the field so the other finalist and I could see the target. I won in what amounted to total darkness.

In 1978, I concentrated my competitive efforts on playing Ultimate Frisbee for

Peter Bloeme playing Ultimate on the East Coast all-star team at the Rose Bowl in 1977.

Cornell University. (Ultimate is a combination of the best of soccer, football and basketball and is played on a 40 by 70 yard field with 25 yard end zones and seven person teams.) The club team consisted almost entirely of college players, yet they invited me to join them. We made it to the finals of the National Ultimate Championship against the Santa Barbara Condors (another club team) and finished second in a highly competitive game.

A Frisbee player since 1969, I became a full-time pro in 1978. Since then I have performed hundreds of times throughout the U.S., Canada and Europe. My professional status led to many television commercials, including a spot for Pepsi-Cola, and numerous interviews on both television and radio, including ESPN, CNN and *"Late Night with David Letterman" (see Professional Appearances page 117 for more on these experiences).* I also created a Frisbee show that I perform at schools, camps, amusement parks, fairs, sport shows, sporting event halftimes and shopping malls. Having amassed a collection of over 3,000 flying discs of all shapes, colors and sizes *(see back cover photo for a partial glimpse).* I have even designed and patented a high performance flying disc. Still, my proudest accomplishment is raising and training Whirlin' Wizard, the 1984 World Champion and Hall of Fame Frisbee dog.

Whirlin' Wizard

No matter where I performed as a Frisbee professional, people would always ask me if I had a Frisbee dog. My typical answer was, "No, I don't. It's just too difficult traveling with one."

Then, in 1982, on a cross-country drive from Seattle to New York, I pondered additions and changes that I would make in my Frisbee show for the coming season. This is when I first started to think seriously about getting a dog. I "tossed" the idea around, picturing what it would have been like having a dog the previous year. Would I have missed out on anthing, lived where I did? During the long drive, I had a lot of time to think through those questions and my feelings were positive. I enjoyed the idea of having a dog to travel with as well as a Frisbee partner to work with and take care of. By that time, I had just about decided to get a dog, but nutrition was one remaining concern. I flipped on the television one night in a Montana motel room and the Westminster Dog Show came on. I watched as a veterinarian discussed healthy food for dogs. After seeing the show, I became aware that there are many good commercial foods now avail-

1984 World Champion Wizard at three months of age

able for dogs. On the rest of my drive I thought about the specifics of acquiring, training, traveling with and feeding a dog.

My first decision was what breed to select. Because of my travel schedule, I decided not to get a large dog. From my familiarity with Ashley Whippet, I began to research Whippets. I called the American Kennel Club (AKC) in New York City and they gave me the name and telephone number of the secretary of a Whippet club.

When I spoke with her she immediately asked, "Why are you interested in getting a Whippet?" I told her I wanted to train one for catching Frisbees. She sounded appalled and asked me how I could think of doing such a thing. She went on to tell me that they were fragile little animals and that one of her dogs broke a leg just running and playing in the back yard. I felt like mentioning to her that sometimes physical weaknesses of "purebred" dogs are due to their being bred or inbred solely for their appearance.

I was annoyed, but continued by asking her if she had ever heard of Ashley Whippet. She answered "Of course." She had seen him perform live and told me she was concerned every time he jumped. Alex Stein, Ashley's owner, laughed when I told him the story. He told me that Ashley had never been injured in the 12 years he competed and performed.

I continued my quest for a dog. After much research, thought and reflection, I selected a Border Collie. The determining factor was seeing three-time World Finalist Jendi Holmes' exciting Border Collies in action. Border Collies are purebred sheepherding dogs originally from Scotland, usually black and white and are fully recognized as a breed by the International Sheep Dog Association. They are medium-sized dogs bred for intelligence, stamina and obedience. Besides, I liked their appearance.

Once I made my choice I discovered an advertisement in Dog World Magazine for three month old Border Collie pups in Gettysburg, Pennsylvania. While driving to the Pacific Northwest from New York on tour, I stopped to look at them. It was winter and they were outside in a dog house. They didn't seem to mind the cold and were having a grand time jumping on each other, play fighting and rolling around in the snow. There were three males to choose

Wizard at eight months during his first professional show at Shea Stadium in 1983.

from. The first one saw me and ran away, arguably a smart move on his part, but unacceptable to me as I took it personally. The remaining two were both very friendly. I finally chose the smaller one because he was less aggressive, yet very responsive, bright eyed and bushy tailed.

I named him Whirlin' Wizard and he thinks he has it easy—his job is just to "herd" Frisbees. I kid him now and then that he should appreciate me or I'll make him get a real job, with lots of sheep.

From the first day, Wizard has been a delight. He started out as a little soft, fluffy pup with what looked like huge nuclear-powered paws. He is now a fully grown and a fully recognized World Class, World Champion and Hall of Fame Frisbee dog. Audiences only see the result of our efforts and comment on his amazing abilities. What they don't realize is how much practice time is involved.

I began to train Wizard immediately by feeding him out of a Frisbee, which I still do. He caught his first Mini Frisbee, about three inches in diameter, at 14 weeks. At that age, I didn't want to use a full-sized disc and take the chance of damaging his teeth or knocking his head off. I added Wizard to my professional shows when he was just 16 weeks old.

At the age of 8 months, Wizard made his professional sporting debut at Shea Stadium between games of a double header for the New York Mets (vs. Philadelphia Phillies) with over 40,000 spectators. He performed like a true

Peter Bloeme and Wizard entertaining crowds at the 1990 Come 'N Get It World Finals.

professional. I know that we didn't make a big "hit" with the New York Mets until after the performance, because Wiz got sick before the show in one of their offices. As I cleaned it up, I realized he must have been a little nervous.

Wizard has never had any "formal" obedience training, but as a foundation for all of his Frisbee stunts I have taught him all the standard commands: sit, stay, down, heel. He learned to obey through both voice and hand signals, making him, in a way, bilingual. When he was a pup, I worked with him four times a day for 15 minutes. Before his retirement we would work about 30 minutes a day—every day, whether it was raining, snowing or sunny. The reason for practicing in all types of weather conditions is that I never knew if we would be required to perform or compete in less than ideal conditions. At one years' canine world finals, for example, a recent rain shower left the ground wet. There was a top dog that day that didn't perform to her potential because she didn't like the wet ground.

Wizard doesn't consider Frisbee work but play, which he loves. All I have to do is say the word "Frisbee" and his ears perk up, his head tilts sideways and he stands motionless. Or as Delta Air Lines' Cynthia Mullennix puts it, *"Wizard comes as close to smiling as a dog can."* When I pick up a Frisbee or even a ball, stick or other toy, he crouches down and stares at the object. Believe it or not, this means he's ready to play. The hard work for me came in channelling this excitement and energy into his becoming a top competitor and performer.

One drawback of owning a sheep-herding dog is the amount of exercise required to keep him happy. If Wizard doesn't get a good workout every day he will drive himself and anyone else around crazy by trying to get volunteers to play with him. This breed simply has a ton of energy. Some dogs chew on an old shoe. Sheep dogs start chewing at one end of a couch and finish at the other. Some dogs dig holes, but sheep dogs excavate! In fact, my current puppy, Magic, is working on a link-up with the Euro tunnel.

Some weekends when I played the team flying disc game Ultimate, my team might play three games. Naturally, before and after each game, Wizard ran wild on the field seeking any human willing to throw him his beloved toy. It is quite a sight to see one dog amid 20 players running, jumping, catching and seemingly never tiring. Yet, by the end of the day when we got in the car, he would lie down and immediately go to sleep. When we got home he would pull himself together stiffly, stagger up the stairs and plop down in his favorite spot. Just when I started to think that taking him to Ultimate was a great way of tiring him out, he would push one of his toys onto my feet, crouched, eager and expecting me to play. Amazing!

One of our most memorable experiences took place at an elementary school. Wizard is very obedient, except he doesn't always obey the command "stay" (he loves Frisbees and children too much). So after he performs, I put his leash on him and have someone hold onto him for the remainder of my show.

At this elementary school, when it was time to find someone to hold him, I turned around and asked the closest adult (who happened to be the principal) to hold Wizard. Actually, I didn't ask but just walked over and handed him Wiz's leash and continued my presentation. I didn't know why at the time, but many of the adults teachers and parents laughed. After the first show, the PTO (Parent Teacher Organization) president told me the reason for the laughter—the principal was afraid of dogs, so I made a mental note not to pick him during the next show.

Imagine my surprise during the second show when I turned to look for an adult to hold Wizard the same principal came running up and took him. After the demonstration he spoke to me at length. It turned out that he had a daughter who loved animals and he was considering getting her a dog, possibly a Border Collie, all because of Wizard.

One of the most frequently asked questions is "How long did it take to teach him?" Because Wizard knows so much, I have to ask "Teach him what?" It took different amounts of time to learn every trick he knows, and he is always learning. I answer by giving his present age and explain that he is continuously working on new things. Every day I try to find something new to challenge him. For example, once I put his favorite basketball in my rope hammock. After a bit of coaching and practice he learned how to bounce it out from the middle, not an easy task from a dog's perspective.

Now that I have provided some background information on myself and Wizard, it is time to look into some of the considerations one needs to take into account before acquiring a dog and teaching him Frisbee.

Peter Bloeme making a long distance throw to Wizard at a Washington Redskin's football halftime in 1986.

Associated Press sports feature award winning photograph by Jeff Carlick: 1984 World Champions Peter Bloeme and Whirlin' Wizard.

Five-time World Finalist Donna Schoech and Charity

Key Canine Considerations

There are many things to consider before you actually begin to look for a Frisbee dog. This is NOT a quick decision that should be taken lightly. If acquiring a puppy, you can expect to spend 15 years, or more, with your friend. Do not get a dog because of a passing fancy or simply to please your children. A dog is a big responsibility and a puppy needs constant care and attention. NEVER give a dog as a gift without asking the recipient first. It is incredibly sad to see dog shelters swell soon after the holiday season with pups that were given on impulse and who outgrew their cuteness. Keep in mind that your dog will depend on you for shelter, food, entertainment and love for his lifetime. Despite those responsibilities, I believe the effort is well worth the love, dedication, loyalty, companionship and protection received in return.

Selecting A Dog

Each breed has different physical characteristics, inherited qualities and weaknesses such as size, intelligence, speed, stamina, agility, jumping ability and intensity. Breeds with long snouts and long legs, such as German Shepherds, Labrador Retrievers and Border Collies, have a better chance of catching a Frisbee than snub-nosed or small dogs such as Bulldogs, Pekingese,

The 1990 Come 'N Get It World Finalists in Washington, D.C.

27

Basset Hounds, Bloodhounds and Dachshunds. These dogs are not well suited to Frisbee play due to their physical limitations. Other elements should be considered: Do you have children, need a dog for protection or simply have preferences for one breed or another? Once you make a selection, part of your responsibility as a dog owner and trainer is to learn to recognize and work with your dog's particular characteristics and special qualities. For example, a hound will be a great tracker, a working dog will be tireless, a hunter will be focused, etc. A good book for investigating various breeds is *Simon & Schuster's Guide To Dogs*, listed in the Appendix.

Purebred dogs can be found through advertisements in your local newspaper, or through magazines such as *Dog World* and *Dog Fancy* and even at animal shelters. If you decide to select one of these, I recommend that you also buy some books on the breed you select. They contain useful information from which you will certainly benefit.

If you prefer you can adopt from an animal shelter. Most shelters offer beautiful dogs for little or no money. The all-American mutt can be a great selection as long as he has the physical characteristics necessary for Frisbee. Four former world canine Frisbee champions were rescued from the pound. With all the unwanted dogs available, saving a dog from the pound can be an especially rewarding experience.

World Finalists Manny Rodriguez and Pawcolo

One of the first things to do after getting a dog is to get a collar and proper identification with his name and your name, address and telephone number imprinted thereon. Have him wear the collar at ALL times, even in the house. If, by accident, you become separated from your dog, an identification tag could be a lifesaver.

Health

When you do get a dog, make sure that he is healthy, lively, friendly and energetic. Before selecting a purebred, research that breed at your public library or local book store. The information available should inform you of any health-related concerns.

It is imperative that your dog be healthy before attempting any strenuous Frisbee activity. Since this is a number one priority, discuss Frisbee training with your veterinarian and have him or her examine your pet regularly. Keep your dog dewormed and keep all his immunizations (such as rabies and parvo) current. Remember, your dog can't tell you if he isn't feeling well, so you must develop the ability to asses his physical and mental condition. Learn to be observant. Notice if your dog is eating properly, check his stools for any discharges or worms, inspect for body odor, broken nail/tooth, etc. While petting your dog, you may feel bumps or lacerations, notice unusual hair loss, parasites, etc. These are all warning signs which should be investigated further.

Early exposure to Frisbee is one thing but this is ridiculous!

Fleas are a problem, especially in warmer climates, but with baths, dips and bombs they can be controlled. I do not recommend the use of flea collars for animals. Think twice before placing a collar around your dog's neck that contains chemicals which, according to the manufacturer, are hazardous to humans. Many veterinarians believe that they may do more harm than good. If you do decide to use one at least remove the collar when giving your dog a bath or letting him swim. The flea-killing chemicals used are intensified by water and are concentrated around your dog's head.

Teeth

If you begin with a puppy, prepare yourself for the nightmare of TEETHING. Take this as a warning: A pup is like an infant and will put everything and anything into his mouth. The difference is that infants don't have pincer-like teeth that can tear cloth, run hose, eat one shoe out of every pair of shoes in the house and destroy the newspaper better than the government can shred classified information.

What you can do to alleviate the situation is to buy chew-toys (by the gross if necessary), including leather bones, rubber bones, balls, etc. If you think your dog will like it—get it. However, do not give your dog an old pair of shoes or socks. Think of it this way: How is your dog going to know an old pair of shoes from a favorite new pair? Avoid giving your dog real bones as these can cause severe intestinal blockage or damage due to splintering.

Also, keep an eye on your dog when he is chewing. It is easy to assume that your dog is happily chewing something you approve of, only to look down and find out it is not so. The genetic makeup of puppies suggests anything within "mouth range" is fair game. Can we help it if that item happens to be a 220 volt dishwasher cord? The answer is yes, I hope.

Since a pup has baby teeth, do not start throwing any big or hard toys, including Frisbees, for him to catch until his adult teeth are in (around 6 months). It is important for his puppy teeth to come in and drop out naturally so that the adult teeth also will come in properly. Incidentally, your dog's teeth will need to be cleaned by the veterinarian periodically, as dogs can contract gum disease similar to humans. Regular cleanings will prevent early tooth decay and subsequent loss.

When your dog is an adult, his teeth will wear down with play. This is normal and is not something to be overly concerned about, but, have your veterinarian check on this from time-to-time. As the tooth wears down the nerve should recede, preventing the tooth from causing your dog any pain. Avoid using dirty or sandy discs; this will lessen the problem. A dirty disc is tantamount to using revolving sandpaper on your dog's teeth every time he makes a catch.

You may notice that your dog seems to gulp his food without chewing. Since a dog's digestion does not begin in the mouth as it does with humans, it's only important that food passes down his throat to his stomach. (It is interesting to note that your dog does not need to have teeth to eat unless he hunts for his food.)

Nutrition

I feel that too many dog owners, doctors and veterinarians do not give enough thought to improper diet as the underlying cause of many health problems for both people and dogs. Since you are responsible for your dog's health, you must select a nutritious and healthy brand of food.

Here are some items to keep in mind. A poor diet can seriously hurt your dog's health and shorten his life span. The best food for your dog is not necessarily the most expensive, as nutritional quality does not always go hand-in-hand with price.

I do not recommend feeding your dog table scraps. They are usually high in fat and will be as unhealthy for your dog's heart and circulatory system as they are for yours. Instead, look for a name-brand pet food, such as Come 'N Get It, with the words "complete and balanced," or "provides 100% nutrition" printed on the package. That way you'll ensure that your dog receives adequate nutrition to support life and promote healthy offspring. Finally, check with your veterinarian to see if your dog requires a normal diet, or a high protein diet because of the amount of exercise he gets.

Above all, do not overfeed your dog! A trim animal is a happy and healthy one. More

Good nutrition is important.

pet owners doom their animals to early deaths by overfeeding than from any other cause. There are no excuses for a fat dog! We may not be able to control what goes into our mouths, but we certainly can regulate what goes into theirs. Dogs still have some of their old instincts such as thinking they need to eat all they can whenever they can. They beg and look forlorn. Don't give in!

Mike Miller and Pro begin their routine with a sit command. This provides time to gather one's thoughts and settle down

You should be able to run your hands over you dog's rib cage and feel his ribs. There also should be some definition between your dog's rib cage and his abdomen. Check with your veterinarian for more specifics.

I also do not recommend "free feeding." This is where you leave food out so that whenever your dog wants to he can eat. Whether your dog competes or just works out, it is better for him to be on a set schedule. That way you can monitor how much he eats and this will provide you a clue as to how he feels. I do recommend that you ALWAYS leave water out for your dog. In the summer, make sure your dog's water is put in a cool or shady area because water left in the hot sun can easily become undrinkable.

While an occasional uncooked solid (others can splinter) soup bone may be good for his teeth, avoid getting in the habit of rewarding your dog with "treats" for obedience. Your dog should perform because he loves you, loves what he does and appreciates your praise. Alex Stein, trainer of Ashley Whippet, calls this "the enthusiasm factor." "The opportunity to catch the Frisbee is its own reward," he says.

Naming Your Dog

When you are ready to choose a name, give it some thought. Remember, your dog will have that name for the rest of his life. Once, when I was performing at a school, a teacher's aide approached me. While she petted Wizard, she told me how she loved dogs and had named one of her's "Stupid," because as a pup it would sleep on the paper and wet on the floor. Her statement was staggering. Believe it or not, paper training is not genetic. Wild dogs do not intuitively look for paper to wet on.

My point is that you should seriously consider the name you give your dog, as it will affect how you and your friends relate to and view him. Also, remember that dogs are born "stupid" in the ways of man. It is up to us to educate them and if they fail, it is usually our fault. My dog seems more like a Whirlin' Wizard

Sas Peters bathes Jake in a horse stall.

every day. Your dog may seem more like an Air Major, Leaping Luke, Aerial Annie, Hyper Hank, Bouncin' Boo or even a Gilbert, Zach, Dink or Casey. But by naming your dog Stupid, how do YOU think he will turn out?

Grooming

Grooming is very important for your dog's health and good looks. The effort needed to groom your dog depends entirely on what breed you have. Therefore, I suggest that you ask your veterinarian for specifics.

I brush Wizard three times a week. I simultaneously examine his coat for ticks and fleas, his nails for length, his ears for dirt and mites and check his teeth for tartar buildup. Tartar can be seen as a hard, yellow coating on a dog's normally white teeth. It causes the gums to become red and inflamed and leads to gum disease that can in turn lead to the loss of healthy teeth. Although the use of dry food and dog biscuits can reduce the speed and amount of the buildup, a thorough cleaning done by a veterinarian is recommended regularly.

I bathe Wizard when it looks like he needs it, though normally not more than once a month, or so. Bathing too frequently can lead to dry skin.

Nails

I know that nails are a part of grooming but this subject has always been a pet peeve of mine. Some people are under the misconception that a dog's nails will wear down enough by themselves through normal day-to-day activity. This is only PARTIALLY true for a dog that works out a lot. Regardless, a dog's nails do not usually wear down evenly. Additionally, dew-claws (thumb nails) require special care. Dogs that get less daily exercise definitely need nail care. Neglect in this area can cause your dog to hobble due to severe pain or may result in an injury to you in play. Don't subject your dog to this neglect, as you can easily trim his nails at home.

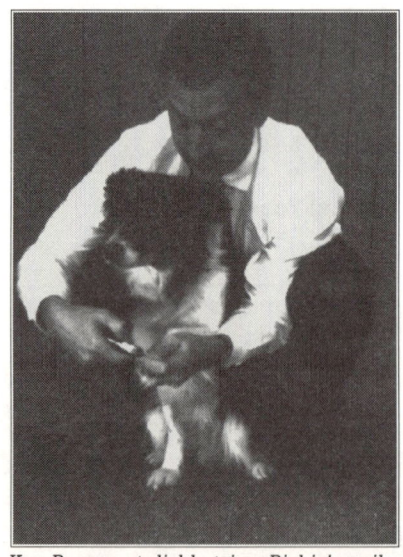

Ken Pogson stylishly trims Richie's nails.

1986 World Champions Chris Barbo and Kato

World Finalists Spencer Huender and Tasha

To trim your dog's nails you will need a dog nail clipper which is available at any pet store. If your dog has translucent nails you can see the quick, the darker or pinkish area inside. Your dog's nails need clipping when they extend beyond the quick. They should not, however, be cut TO the quick. If you ask your veterinarian to show you how, I'm sure he or she will be happy to demonstrate the proper technique. If you cut into the quick by accident it will be painful to your dog and will cause bleeding. Control a small cut with a styptic pencil or a small amount of inert powder such as talcum or flour. If your dog's nails are all black you must exercise caution and concentrate only on the thinner tips.

Obedience

In the following Basic Training Techniques section I have outlined two methods that I feel have merit and are useful with Frisbee training. If you have never trained a dog before, you might consider taking your dog to obedience school. Many good books are also available on the subject. I highly recommend the *Complete Book of Dog Training* and *Super-Training Your Dog* by Jo and Paul Loeb, both listed in the Appendix.

Each dog responds differently, but every trainer needs to include love, understanding, consistency and patience in a training regimen and in daily interaction with their dog.

It's only human to want your dog to be obedience trained and a Frisbee star overnight, but patience is the key to success. Keep initial workout sessions short, possibly as short as a few throws. Stop BEFORE your dog gets tired so that he doesn't get the impression that playing Frisbee is a chore. Work on one trick at a time or you may confuse your pet.

Once your dog has mastered a trick, start a new one while continuing the old one. Each dog is different—some have fast stages of growth and development while others have slow ones. It's important to learn to recognize this and to train accordingly.

Begin your dog's education as early as possible, starting as young as three months old. Remember to always train in a fun, friendly and relaxed manner. At an early age your dog will have a very short attention span, so plan accordingly. Training should seem like a big game. Before your dog is three months old let him be a pup with few responsibilities.

I don't want to give the impression that you have to start with a puppy, but, it's sometimes easier if you do. An adult dog, of any age and good health, can learn new tricks; it just takes a little longer because he may be set or "corrupted" in his ways. For those older dogs not accustomed to strenuous physical activity, it is a good idea to encourage them to play at their own pace. When in doubt, consult your veterinarian!

Commands

Consistency is very important: always remember to use the same word for a particular command. I said "word" because it's important not to confuse your dog with long, drawn-out commands. It's easier for your dog to hear, differentiate and follow single-word commands. For example, say, "Down" not "Fluffy, please go lie down." Also, whatever you say, use an animated voice with a lot of inflection.

Three words that cannot be stressed enough are "No," "Down" and "Come." The reason I say this is because they can save your dog's life. For example "No" could be used to stop your dog from eating a sharp bone, while "Down" or "Come" might be used to prevent your dog from running into the street.

Sometimes the commands "Down" and "Off" get confused but they have completely different meanings and are important to differentiate. "Down" means lie down and "Off" means get off whatever you are on. Once, early in our relationship, my wife Lynn wanted Wizard to get off the couch and kept yelling, "Down" at him. He just lay there. When I arrived, I told him, "Off," and he jumped down. Lynn just glared at me. Once you have come up with various com-

Your dog will usually go for the muddiest spot around to cool off. Nestle proudly demonstrates.

mands, make sure that others in contact with the dog know what they are.

One last word of advice is be careful in choosing your release word. A release word is one that you use to tell your dog to relax. For instance, when you tell your dog to stay, you also need a command to tell him that he can now do as he pleases. You also might use a release word to tell your dog that he can get out of the car or cross the street. Some books recommend the word "Okay," but since this word is used so often in daily communication, a dog can be released unintentionally. There are two options for choosing a release word. The first is to choose a word that you would rarely use in normal conversation. The second is to make up a word that would never come up in conversation. I use a made up word, "Kea," pronounced "Key-ah."

The Gary Larson cartoon *(see above)* illustrates what your dog hears and what he understands. In most cases, dogs do not have the intellect or comprehension skills of man, so keep it simple for them.

Basic Training Techniques

For most of Wizard's training I used a common technique I call guiding. For example, with the sit command, I would gently push his hindquarters to the floor until he sat, while saying, "Sit." I then kept him in the sitting position and praised him for being so smart. This is very important. I praised him although the whole process was controlled by me. Any time you give your dog love and attention he will try to please you to receive more of the same. He will work at figuring out what pleases you and will continue to do it.

I can't stress enough the importance of rewarding your dog both verbally (by praising him) and physically (by petting him). I am not a strong believer in using food treats to train animals. At times during initial training you might consider a food treat, but generally it is not necessary. In fact, it can be detrimental to a dog's performance. He can get to the point where he will refuse to work without a treat. The proper way is to get him to WANT to perform and play because he enjoys it and because it pleases you so much.

Praise your dog from the time he begins to get the idea until the time he masters the trick, and before you know it, he will be doing it correctly. Wizard can catch easily, but I still acknowledge his accomplishments verbally and physically to let him know I am pleased. Dogs thrive on love, attention and recognition. I have never given Wizard a food treat of any kind for doing a trick. I just pet him and say words like, "Good boy, way to go, Wiz." Plenty of praise and the fun of the game will keep your dog very happy and playing in top form.

An alternative is the patience method, where you wait until your dog does what you want without pulling, pushing or coaching. Using the same example as above, I would wait until Wizard sat, then say, "Sit" a few times and congratulate him for desired behavior.

I have used this method successfully many times. It was good for house-breaking. I would take Wizard outside and when he relieved himself I would say, "Out." I kept doing this until I could say, "Out" and he knew it was time to eliminate. This skill is more valuable than it may seem at first. For example, before competition or a demonstration I would walk him and say, "Out" so that he wouldn't have to stop in the middle of his routine for a nature break. This prevented both embarrassment to me and an interruption in our performance.

Another way this method can be used is with the command "Speak." Just wait until your dog's favorite someone (possibly the mailman) shows up at your door. When your dog starts to bark, say, "Speak." After doing this a few times he will have learned to speak on command.

The patience method is also apparent in the way Wizard learned the back flip. I got Wizard to jump backward with an intentionally crooked throw and when he went for the catch, I'd say, "Back." After a while he got the idea that when I said back, he should make a back flip to catch the throw. This was a trick that I couldn't easily guide him through, yet it was something that was consistent and predictable.

Every so often it is a good idea to test your dog and put him on notice that you will not always be using the same order in your commands. In demonstrations I would tell Wizard to sit, then lie down, then roll-over at the beginning of our routine. It got so familiar to Wizard that when we were in a show situation and I said, "Sit" at the beginning of the show he would sit, lie down and roll-over in one continuous motion. Dogs can be TOO smart at times. Keep your dog honest: mix up the order on occasion. The next time I said, "Down, Sit, Down, Roll." He was so embarrassed when he did it wrong that he started to listen again.

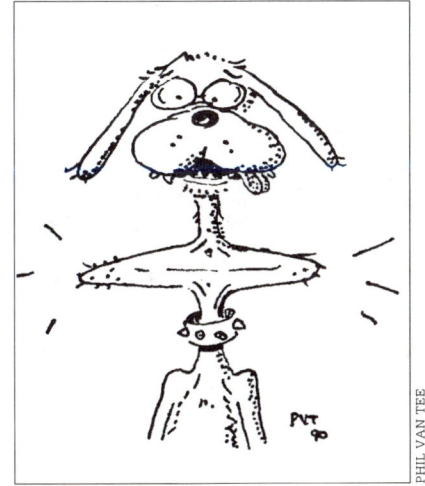

Common Injuries

Most of the time, when you use common sense, playing Frisbee with your dog is safe. Still, there are two things

Three-time World Champion Bouncin' Boo

that commonly occur that you should be aware of. A sharp edge on a disc can cut a dog's lip, tongue or gums during play. Even when your disc is new at the beginning of your session, it can become sharp during play.

Also, your dog will occasionally bite his tongue. This is not surprising since PEOPLE often bite their tongues when eating, and your dog is using his mouth to catch a moving disc! This will more likely occur after your dog is hot and panting. Since a dog's tongue is used to keep himself cool, he sticks it out when he is hot. Then the Frisbee comes by and "bam!" He inadvertently closes his mouth on the disc without pulling his tongue completely back in his mouth. When this happens his tongue may bleed, but some cool water should stop it quickly. Speak with your veterinarian if you are concerned about excessive bleeding.

Dallas Dog and Disc club member Bethe Lehman enjoying a quiet moment with her dog Guthrie.

The two worst causes of injuries are not Frisbee related; they are car accidents and dog fights. Both can almost always be prevented with common sense, proper obedience training and the use of a leash.

Discipline

NEVER HIT YOUR DOG! If your dog does not obey you, it is probably your fault for not teaching him properly. I realize that training can be occasionally frustrating, but it is both dangerous to your dog's health and unproductive to his cooperation and understanding if you use violence. I'm sure the same could be said about children. You want a dog that respects you, not fears you. If you must punish your dog, there are various, safe methods such as using a stern vocal tone and level. This form of punishment usually works well. At the extreme, if your dog commits a serious offense, such as something that may endanger his life, you may have to resort to grabbing the back of your dog's neck, shaking and scolding him. This is apparently very similar to what a mother dog would do to scold a pup. It looks a lot worse to bystanders than it is, but it gets a dog's attention.

Four-time World Finalists Mark Wood and Zach

Frisbee Basics

One of the most important things in training your dog to play and enjoy Frisbee is, surprisingly enough, for YOU to throw adequately and accurately. Remember, you are a member of a team and it isn't fair to let your partner down. Developing your throwing skills will enhance your dog's catching abilities. I have often seen dogs with great potential do poorly in competition due to their owners' consistently bad throws. Even Wizard has looked less than a champ because of throwing errors made by friends and celebrities (sometimes even by me). I recommend that you learn to throw before playing Frisbee with your dog so you won't confuse him or give him bad catching habits.

Disc Selection

There are many differences in flying discs and because of their various colors, shapes, sizes and materials, some are obviously more suited to canine play than others. Discs can be made out of plastic, cloth, rubber or fabric. As a collector with over 3,000 different flying discs and as an owner of a disc patent, I have seen just about every disc imaginable. The Fastback Frisbee disc by Wham-O currently offers the best overall characteristics for play with adult dogs. Weighing nine ounces and made of polyethylene plastic, the disc is light and has a well-rounded and smooth rim. Fastbacks are typically used as promotional give-away items and are not readily available for sale in stores. The next best disc to use is Wham-O's Regular Model (inexpensive and available almost everywhere). Whichever you choose, remember that your dog will catch the Frisbee in his mouth with his TEETH.

Original Fastback Frisbee

Puppies have sharp but fragile needle-like teeth. Obviously, it is not a good idea to get the monster sized disc out to play with your pup. You want his adult teeth to safely grow in naturally with proper development and strength. I started Wizard with a Mini Frisbee which is three inches in diameter, because I didn't want to knock his teeth out. Then we moved up to a very soft, 5-inch diameter disc and finally to the common, nine-inch size when he was 6 months old. I don't recommend using the large model, except as a food dish and for basic training until his adult teeth grow in.

Dogs are colorblind, so the color of your disc is important mainly for creating contrasting images. To a dog, some background colors will look the same as the Frisbee you are using, so make it easy on him by using a disc that will stand out from its surroundings. For example, blue and red would be my favorite choices for use in an open area on a overcast day. A light colored disc should stand out well against a blue sky. At dusk, when colors are fading, humans start to have trouble seeing (without lights), but dogs can still see well.

Speaking of sight, keep in mind that because of his head height, your dog has a different perspective on everything than you. He most often focuses on objects at his eye level and therefore has to look up to see the same object that you or I can see straight ahead. This may help you understand why your dog will or will not do certain things. Keep this in mind during training. For example, the reason your dog may not jump over something is that he can't see what awaits him on the other side. So, at first, position your dog so that he has a full view of his surroundings.

Dogs have better peripheral vision than we do—up to 120 degrees. This means that he will be more adept at spotting and catching throws off to the side than you might think possible. This capability is invaluable in this sport.

Gimmicks

There are many flying disc "gimmicks" on the market; some are even specifically geared toward dog owners. They may be great for adult play and collecting, but generally I recommend that you stick with reliable, safe Fastbacks for your dog. The Gumabone Frisbee Flying Disc is the only exception. I have devoted the next section to this disc.

I do not recommend the Whistle Disc for canine play. The reason I mention it at all is because I have seen it advertised in catalogs catering to the dog owner. This disc whistles as it flies, making it fun for people but not for dogs. Three evenly spaced whistles are built into the rim, just where your dog catches it. If your dog

The Whistle Disc

Tara jumps for joy at the 1990 Come 'N Get It Western Regional Championship.

grabs a Whistle Disc in the air his mouth or tongue could easily be cut by the whistles in the edge. If you must buy it, keep it as a collectable, do not use it around pets or children.

I also recommend avoiding the Aerobie. Lately, there has been much talk about how easy this product is to throw and how far it flies. In fact, I was asked to write a book about it. There is no question that it flies far and is fairly easy to throw. I don't recommend it for general canine play, because of its extreme narrow profile and high speed. However, for use as a prop as shown in photo above, it can be an interesting variation for short tosses.

Three-time World Finalist Jendi Holmes and Scotland demonstrating short throws with an Aerobie.

Finally, "scented" discs have been introduced for dogs by Wham-O and other disc manufacturers. Although this is an interesting variation on air pollution, you may wonder why anyone would make a scented disc. Apparently the research and development wizards at these companies decided that if a disc were made that smelled like food, you would be more likely to buy it, thinking your dog would love you for it. On the contrary, it probably will drive you both crazy. Besides, you don't want him to eat the thing, just catch it. Again I recommend that you use a "dull," unscented Fastback or Regular Model Frisbee; sources for discs are listed in the Appendix.

Gumabone Frisbee Flexible Flying Disc

The one "gimmick" disc that I have come across that seems beneficial to the dog owner is the Gumabone Frisbee Flexible Flying Disc by Nylabone Products (hereafter referred to as the Gumadisc). My dogs have "soft mouths" which mean they try to cradle the disc when making a catch thereby not doing much damage to it. On the other hand, Gilbert, the 1989 World Champion has as hard a mouth as they come. So I asked his owner/trainer Jeff Perry, to do a review of this disc for "Flying Dog News," a newsletter for Frisbee dog enthusiasts. (It is no longer published.) With his permission, I am reprinting it here:

"Professional bird dog trainers go to great lengths to ensure that their dogs have 'soft mouths' (a dog with a soft mouth retrieves birds without further damage). Some trainers use dummy birds wrapped in barbed wire to reinforce the idea in the minds of young 'trainees' that birds are to be handled with care. Unfortunately, there is very little that a Frisbee dog owner can do to train his dog to catch with a soft mouth.

"Although some dogs snare Frisbees gently, most of them seem to take great pleasure in reducing a flying disc to its chemical components as quickly as possible. For these dogs, Nylabone Products has developed a dog-resistant line of discs called Gumabone Frisbee Flexible Flying Discs or Gumadisc.

"The Gumadisc is made of a tear and puncture resistant plastic that achieves strength, not from its toughness or rigidity but from a unique molecular structure that is similar to the mouth guards used by professional boxers and football players.

"Nylabone Products makes a variety of discs. They come in three sizes (three and a half, five and nine inches) and in two styles: molded bone on top and plain. In addition, they are available in two materials, one hard and rigid and the other soft and flexible. Each disc comes with an instructional booklet detailing various training methods that looks, not surprisingly, like the Ashley Whippet Invitational's training booklet. I do not recommend the models with the raised bone protruding from the top of the disc or the models made out of the stiff and rigid material, because of the potential for mouth and tooth injuries. According to Nylabone Products, the 'bone top' disc was designed to help dogs in picking up discs from the ground. Perhaps the best use for the 'bone top' model, then, would be to train beginning dogs who can't catch a disc while it is airborne. I see no use at all for the rigid model. By the way, for those dog owners who include swimming as part of their dog's training, it is important to note that Gumadiscs will NOT float.

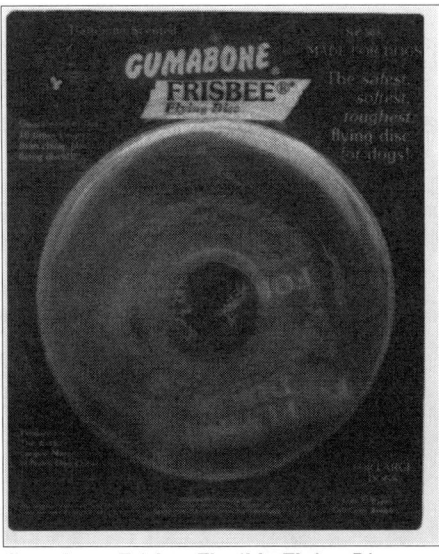

Gumabone Frisbee Flexible Flying Disc.

"As a test subject I used my dog Gilbert, a short-haired Pointer who weighs approximately 50 pounds. Gilbert has the proven capability to reduce a Fastback Frisbee to fragments in minutes. Over the past four years his nimble teeth have shortened the life spans of several hundred discs.

"I began the test by engaging in a typical practice session lasting approximately 30 minutes. It consisted of short and long throws at various angles and spins, also an assortment of standard tricks. After practice I carefully examined the Gumadisc. Remarkably, it showed virtually no damage or wear. For general fetching and catching purposes, the Gumadisc proved highly resistant to damage.

"I also found an additional, perhaps less obvious benefit of the Gumadisc. Its relative flexibility and softness could reduce the likelihood of mouth injuries caused by sharp protruding shards of plastic sometimes present on worn Frisbees.

Small dogs enjoy the sport of canine Frisbee as much as larger ones.

Getting your dog to release the disc is sometimes easier said than done.

1989 World Champion Jeff Perry shows good form and common sense in releasing the disc before Gilbert rips it from his mouth.

"My only complaint about the Gumadisc is probably a bit esoteric. Although this may sound odd, it did not appear to me that my dog, Gilbert, enjoyed the physical act of catching a Gumadisc as much as he enjoys catching a standard Frisbee. The usual solid chomp is replaced by a non-event...silence. Gilbert's catches of the Gumadisc seemed almost timid in comparison with his aggressive grabs of standard plastic discs. Still, timidity not-withstanding, he did catch the Gumadisc as consistently as he catches a standard Frisbee.

"From the thrower's perspective, the Gumadisc takes a little getting used to. The disc that I tested was approximately the same size and weight as a standard Fastback Frisbee. When held, the Gumadisc feels flimsy. Because of the non-rigidity of the plastic, it is difficult to impart much spin on the disc and thus long-distance throws are difficult. Also, many throws are a bit more wobbly than throws with a more rigid disc, but practice with the Gumadisc can smooth out your flights.

"For those dog owners who use the disc in a non-aerodynamic manner (e.g., end-over-end, inverted, etc.) the Gumadisc is somewhat difficult to throw because of its flexibility. Rapid wrist snaps cause it to deform and absorb energy rather than spinning or flipping end-over-end as rapidly as a standard disc would when thrown in an identical manner.

"In conclusion, I feel that it is unlikely that the Gumadisc will replace the standard Wham-O Fastback Frisbee as the disc of choice for the sport of canine Frisbee. Still, as a general purpose training disc, the Gumadisc definitely fills a void and could save a Frisbee dog enthusiast much money over a dog's career."

Frisbee Care And Maintenance

Frisbees generally don't require much care and maintenance, but here are a few tips to improve your game. During practice you should use a towel to keep the disc clean and dry. Alleviating the "slime factor" will help keep your throws consistent.

You'll probably notice that with play, your discs will develop rough and sharp edges. If you leave them that way they can cut your dog's mouth. The remedy is simple: use fine grade sandpaper to smooth the edges after every couple of play sessions. Between practice sessions, I recommend that you wash off the discs so there is no dirt, saliva or sand-

Fastback after a few minutes with Gilbert. (Doggie owner's idea of a NIGHTMARE.)

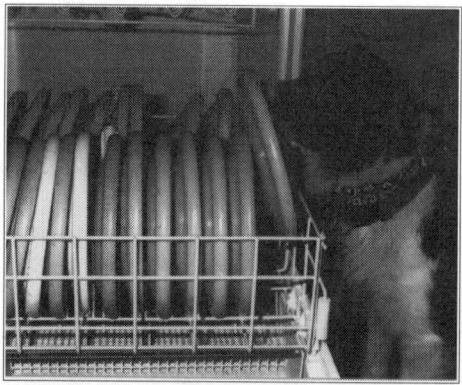

"Really dad, I don't think this one is dirty."

paper grit left on them, making them more sanitary and safer for your dog. This can be done by hand or in the dishwasher.

Of course there are some dogs who insist on putting their teeth through the Frisbee on every throw. For owners with dogs like these there is very little maintenance necessary. After each day of practice they simply throw the discs away (unless they used Gumadiscs). I haven't known anyone who could alter their dog's bite from hard to soft during Frisbee training, so don't encourage it. This is one reason I don't believe in tug-of-war with a disc. Don't give your dog bad habits you will later regret.

Frisbee Aerodynamics

The edge of a flying Frisbee operates under the same scientific principles as an airfoil, meaning it is designed to produce reaction from the air. The concept is simple. The air that passes over the disc travels faster than the air passing underneath, which causes a low pressure area above. The air underneath is not affected by the airfoil, so it moves up to fill this void, causing the disc to rise.

Since the Frisbee spins like a gyroscope, additional properties come into play. The Frisbee not only needs forward motion but also spin for its stability. One or the other is not enough. Just try pushing the disc through the air with no spin. You'll find that it flutters and falls.

The Frisbee cannot accelerate once it has been thrown, so your initial release is critical.

Another consideration is the angle of release. Is the nose (front) of the disc pointed up or down? Too far up and the disc will come back to you. Too far down and it will dive to the ground. What about the side position? Is it angled up or down? If it's too extreme one way or the other, it will either slice or hook. You can experiment with the following elements after you master the basic throws: skips, curves, floaters and distance flights.

When outside forces such as wind and weather conditions come into play, you can see why just one

type of throw can fly so many different ways. Weather cannot be controlled, but you can work with it and take advantage of it. Weather is an element that even the most experienced competitors often overlook.

It appears as if World Finalist Maggy is trying out for a new Come 'N Get It bag.

World Finalist Rhett Butler snags a throw from his owner Jeff Hartshorne.

Throwing

The framework for all throws is similar and includes grip, spin, stance and general elements. Practice the different grips and throws at short distances. As you develop control, increase your distance.

Grip

Use a firm but not tight grip to hold the Frisbee. After you develop a comfortable grip, practice it repeatedly until it becomes second nature. As in golf and tennis, a good grip is paramount to success.

Spin

Always put a good amount of spin on the Frisbee upon release. The more spin, the longer the Frisbee will hold its stability. At first, beginners can simply concentrate on wrist snap. Ideally, however, spin is imparted to a disc through several factors, including proper body position and a snapping motion that originates from a steady stance and progresses through the hips, arm, elbow and finally, the wrist.

Stance

For a proper stance, your feet should be shoulder's width apart with your knees slightly bent and parallel to each other. Your forward shoulder should point toward your target. Start with two-thirds of your weight on your back foot. Then shift it naturally forward to your front foot (leaving one-third of your weight on your back foot) upon release and delivery. Don't lift your back foot off the ground and lunge forward; always keep some weight on each foot.

World Finalist Peter Carlos prepares for his next throw to his dog Baxter.

World Finalists Tom Wehrli and Delta demonstrating a backhand throw.

General Elements

The most important rule to remember when starting out is to keep the Frisbee's flight as flat as possible. The disc will react differently if released angled nose down or up or angled side-to-side.

It is rare that you will find perfect weather conditions (no wind) for practice, unless you have access to an indoor site such as the Pontiac Silverdome. Therefore, always try to throw across the wind, not downwind or upwind. Once you are proficient as a thrower you may choose to throw into the wind for extra float time. However, only attempt this when the wind is steady, otherwise you take the risk of the disc moving up or down suddenly as your dog jumps for it.

At first, practice only short range throws (10 to 15 feet) that are released between waist and shoulder height. GRADUALLY increase the distance of your throws as you succeed at shorter distances. Attempting to increase distance before mastering the basics can cause many technical and mechanical problems through overexertion. You want to make smooth, level and accurate throws and build upon success.

Throws (as described for right handed throwers)

There are many different grips and deliveries. The ones that I explain here will give you a solid foundation of Frisbee basics to practice before you begin training your dog.

Backhand

The backhand throw is a versatile and easy to learn delivery. Once mastered, it can be used for accuracy, distance and trick throws.

I recommend a combination of popular grips called "the Modified Berkeley Power Grip" *(see photos page 53)*. Make a fist with your palm up; open your

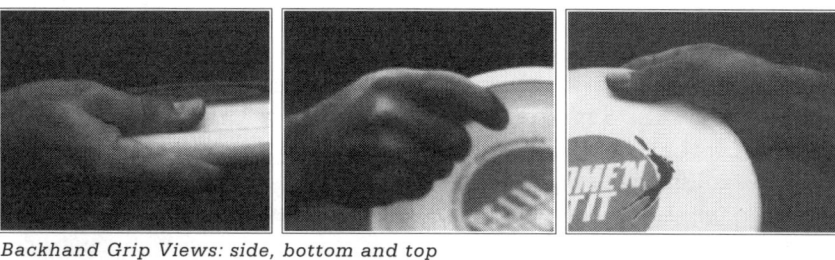

Backhand Grip Views: side, bottom and top

For a straight throw the Frisbee should be released at the angle shown at left or in middle. *This angle is incorrect for a straight throw.*

Backhand Delivery: full motion from beginning to release

thumb to the "hitchhiking" position. Loosen your fingers just enough to slip the Frisbee between your palm and finger tips and place your thumb down on top. This probably will feel awkward. This is called the Berkeley power grip—it is best for pure distance, but it is difficult to control. Now, bring your other hand up and hold the other side of the Frisbee temporarily. Move the fingers of your gripping hand slightly toward your thumb (while trying to maintain as much contact as possible with the inside/bottom rim) until they feel somewhat comfortable. DO NOT go so far as to place your index finger along the outside edge of the Frisbee, doing so would cause you to lose accuracy and control. Now you have the modified grip.

Stand with your right foot forward. Bring the Frisbee back across your body to just above your left side until your arm is as far back as your left shoulder. Your arm should be bent slightly, with your wrist bent inward and the Frisbee held flat.

The throwing motion should be left to right, smooth and even, with a good snap upon release. Do not rotate your wrist from side to side, only forward and backward as if you were doing wrist curls with a dumbbell. Follow through with your right hand (not just the finger) pointing at your target. Keep your eyes forward. If your throw goes to the left of the target you've released it too soon, to the right, too late. Most people fall into the too-late category and hook their throw to the right.

If the disc wobbles, check your grip, speed up your delivery and concentrate on keeping the Frisbee level from your release to your dog's catch.

Roller Delivery: using the backhand grip, release disc on edge.

Roller

For this throw, use the backhand grip. The throwing angle is steep, almost vertical. If you pictured a clock in front of you, the disc would be positioned at the 11 o'clock position. Bring your arm toward your chest and snap your wrist forward and down. Make sure to bend down or kneel close to the ground so that your throw will roll, not bounce. Your release should be perpendicular to the ground. Roller throws are great for introducing puppies or new trainees to the motion of the disc as they are especially easy for canines to see, track and follow.

Upside-Down Slider

This is also an excellent throw for a puppy and is best thrown from a kneeling position. Grip the disc as shown in the photographs on page 55. You may have to move your fingers slightly to get comfortable. Instead of releasing the disc in

Throwing

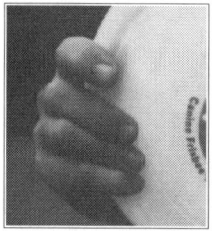 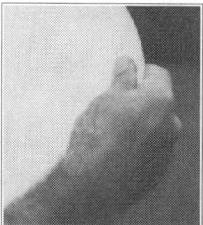  

Upside-down Grip Views: bottom and top   Upside-down Slider: beginning position and release

Upside-down Delivery: the angle upon release should be about 11 o'clock

the air, you throw it flat so that it skims across the ground like a hockey puck. This throw can be used indoors with great success.

Upside-Down

The upside-down throw is great for variety (for you and your dog). It's also challenging and unusual. Since the disc is upside-down, it doesn't float as well in the air, it FALLS. Release the Frisbee at the 11 o'clock position like the roller. Make your throw a little higher so it will flatten out as it falls to your partner.

Advanced Throws

I had originally planned to end my explanation of throws at this point, but since the level of competition has grown tremendously over the past few years, I feel that it is important to mention a few advanced throws that are now commonly used in canine disc play.

Skip

A skip occurs when the disc "bounces" off the ground and back into the air. I don't consider it very useful for Frisbee dogs because it is very difficult to do on

Two-time World Finalist Ron Ellis demonstrates an unusual upside-down delivery to his dog Magg

grass. Still, some people do use the skip in competition for variety. It is difficult for a beginner to learn a skip throw on grass, so practice it on a hard surface first. (Remember, never play with your dog on concrete, asphalt or other hard surfaces for obvious safety reasons.)

Use the backhand grip, but instead of holding and throwing the Frisbee at a level attitude, you throw it with an extreme angle, about 7 o'clock, almost perpendicular to the ground. Most people think that you try to hit the leading or front edge of the Frisbee, but it is actually the side edge that hits. This throw needs a lot of spin and good forward motion. Think of it as a hard curve that hits the ground. This will take some experimentation. Once you have mastered this throw on a hard surface, practice it on short grass where you must throw it harder to get the same effect.

Backhand skip

Sidearm

The sidearm is an advanced, but common throw in which only three fingers are used to grip the disc. Turn the Frisbee upside-down. Make a "peace" or "victory" sign with your first two fingers. Place your middle finger against the inside rim while keeping your first finger flat against the flight plate (the bottom of the disc, not the rim). Grip the top with your thumb. Turn the Frisbee right-side-up. Your last two fingers are bent and used as a guide. This time, stand with your left foot and shoulder toward your partner. The arm motion will be from right to left. Bend your arm in a 90 degree angle and keep your elbow close to your body. Bend your wrist back and then snap it forward. Concentrate on using mostly wrist action rather than arm motion for this throw. Release the Frisbee at 5 o'clock. This one may take a bit of practice.

Sidearm Grip Views: bottom and top

The best use of the basic sidearm throw I've seen is by two-time world finalist Ron Ellis with his dog Maggy. He has a four throw combination where he throws short, 10-yard tosses back and forth to her. He alternates between backhand and sidearm deliveries. One throw is a soft floater

FRISBEE DOGS: How to Raise, Train and Compete

Sidearm Delivery: from beginning to release

that she must leap up to catch. She then races back in the opposite direction and grabs a soft backhand.

Jeff Gabel, a two-time world champion, uses an advanced version of the sidearm throw with great success. He runs toward his dog Casey, who is also running toward him. As his dog gets close to him Gabel jumps up, clears his dog easily and throws a between-the-legs sidearm in the direction the dog is going. Casey seems to kick in the afterburners and takes off after it to make the catch.

Two-Handed

This is an excellent all-round throw for variety and short distances; it gives you tremendous control of the Frisbee's angle.

Explaining this throw in words is more difficult than the throw itself *(see photos below)*. I hope you will be able to use the text and photos to learn it. Open

Two-handed Delivery: from beginning to release

58

Two-time World Champions Jeff Gabel and Casey

Finger tapping

your hands flat and put them together so they are touching in a prayer type position, with fingers pointed up at eye level. Move them apart wide enough to insert the Frisbee so that it rests even with the center point of your middle fingers. Without letting go of the disc, rotate it in a clockwise direction until the back of your right hand is in front of your nose. The disc should still be level. If this is done correctly there should be a little tension. You might even rest the disc slightly on the outside of your left thumb at this point.

To make the throw, push with your right hand and pull with your left, moving the disc in a counter-clockwise motion to give it spin. Simultaneously use your arms to direct the throw above your head.

This throw also can be made in a forward motion by starting with the Frisbee over your head and spinning and pushing the disc forward.

Tapping/Tipping

Technically, tapping belongs in the basics section because it can be combined with the two-handed throw. But it is also an advanced trick. Originally developed in human competition as a unique move for the "freestyle" event, it was used to impress the audience and fellow competitors. Hit the bottom of the disc with your finger as it floats to you during its descent and then make the catch. This can be combined with a two-handed throw over your head and tapped to your dog who makes the catch. For variation, you can do this with different parts of your body. Try tapping the disc with your elbow, knee or foot.

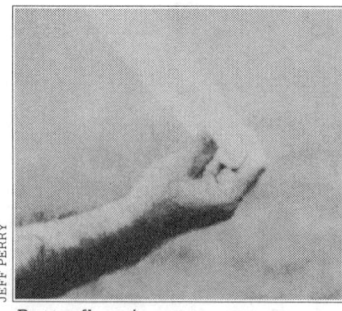

Butterfly grip.

Butterfly

Frisbees are most commonly thrown vertically, horizontally, or upside down. Although the disc flies best these ways, they are not the only options. Popular with the dogs is the butterfly (also known as end-over-end or third world spin) where the disc flips or tumbles to the dog. Again, there are many variations of this throw and variations in the use of it.

Here is the basic throw which you can

Butterfly Delivery: from beginning position to release

expand on later: Hold the Frisbee with your left hand at eye level. Reach under the Frisbee with your right hand to the leading edge so that your four fingers are facing you on top and your thumb is on the bottom. The disc should not be resting deeply in your palm but approximately where your fingers join your hand. Let go of the disc with your left hand so that you have a grip with the right. This is the basic grip. To throw the disc snap down and forward. The disc should go about three or four feet and be flipping end-over-end. *(See Advanced Frisbee Training page 73, to understand how your dog will catch this one.)*

Now that YOU'VE mastered Frisbee throws it's time to teach your DOG!

1980 competitor and dog at the Rose Bowl in Pasadena.

1990 World Champion Lou McCammon and Scooter demonstrating a "Chest" vault.

Basic Frisbee Training

In general, until your dog is about three months old just let him be a puppy without a care in the world. In fact, you may want to wait until that age before getting a dog, since he may need the time with his mother and siblings for proper development.

At three months you may begin housebreaking and teaching basic tricks, including Frisbee play. At six months you can begin training in earnest. And at one year you should have a firm foundation laid so that you and your dog can learn and practice new things together.

Workout Area

At first (and later for variety) you can hold training sessions inside your home. There are usually fewer distractions indoors than there are outside.

After working a short time indoors, your dog will point out all the distractions there are in the room, down to the dust on the floor.

Once you move outside, you shouldn't play on hard dirt, asphalt, concrete, near automobiles or broken glass. Both asphalt and concrete become extremely hot in the summer. Running on these surfaces, even when cool, will tear and damage the pads on your dog's feet. The danger of cars speaks for itself.

For real workouts you will need to go outside to a grassy area that is somewhat level and free of obstacles. A fenced-in back yard is ideal. If you practice in a public park keep in mind a few important considerations. Since your dog is off-leash it's important for him to be under good verbal control because of stray dogs or cars. Also, make sure that your dog has a collar with your name and address in case he gets spooked and runs away. Maintain proper off-leash control so that your dog does not bother those

A safe workout area is important for EVERYONE.

11-week-old Magic sleeping in his favorite water bowl.

around you. This means that you should train him to get along not only with strangers, but to be sociable with other dogs that might be in the area. Whether it is the law in your area or not, clean up after your dog so that you and other dog owners will always be welcome in the park. Be aware of local ordinances that require your dog to be on-leash in certain areas.

One of the best (and safest) workout methods for strengthening and conditioning your dog is with water training. Once your dog has learned to swim, throw his favorite toy (hopefully a Frisbee), into the water so that he has to swim out and bring it back. Repeat this until you feel that he has had a good workout. Occasionally, do this instead of your usual land sessions, especially once your dog has advanced to vaults, etc. Water training is the perfect way to provide low-impact aerobic conditioning without jarring your dog's joints. Don't forget to remove your dog's flea collar before he swims. The flea-killing chemicals used in most collars are intensified by water and can pose a threat to your dog's health in high doses.

A perfect example of using the water for strengthening and conditioning was when Ron Ellis' dog Maggy sustained a non-Frisbee related injury to one of her legs seven weeks before a regional competition. Ron allowed her to rest completely for four weeks. At that point, Ron doubted that she would be ready for the rigors of the tough competition, so with his veterinarian's advice he decided to start Maggy swimming simply for therapy and exercise. Fellow competitors Bob and Marilyn Evans generously offered the use of their pool

1989 World Champion Gilbert demonstrates canine Frisbee water training.

A child's wading pool is great for heat relief.

every day during the week before the competition. Maggy's condition improved dramatically. Although Ron and Maggy could only practice four times in seven weeks, Maggy won the Regional title!

Caution: Many books recommend against having your dog swim in a chlorinated pool because dogs can get sick by drinking the water. Rivers and lakes are better but beware of local hazards such as underwater obstacles, and alligators.

Weather Conditions

Be aware of the temperature where you are working out. Remember, your dog has a fur coat. Whether your dog has short or long hair, it's easy for him to get overheated in warm weather because he cannot sweat (as humans do) to dissipate heat. Panting is the dog's primary method of internal cooling. Never leave your dog locked in a car even with the windows open. On a hot day an automobile can quickly turn into an oven. A dog's normal body temperature is 101.5 degrees and in the summertime even a short stay inside a parked car can be dangerous. For example, the temperature inside your car on an 85 degrees day can reach 102 degrees in only 10 minutes. In 30 minutes, the temperature will reach 120 degrees...and that's with the windows slightly open. A dog can only stand temperatures like these for a very short time before suffering heat stroke or irreparable brain damage.

At the beach there are also considerations you need to keep in mind. According to the Humane Society, dogs should never be taken to the beach between 10 am and 4 pm. That is when the sun's rays are the strongest and dogs are the most susceptible to heat stroke. If you plan to bring your dog with you to the beach, rent an umbrella to help keep him cool. Keep him off the

Three-time World Champion Bouncin' Boo taking a water break.

hot sand; the pads of a dog's feet have just as many nerves as human feet. So if the sand feels hot to you, it will feel hot to your dog.

Dogs love to romp in the surf with a Frisbee, but saltwater is not for drinking. Be sure to bring fresh water from home for him. Saltwater also can dry his skin, so bathe your dog with a mild shampoo when you get home. This will also help remove the embedded sand from his coat. Again, don't forget to remove your dog's flea collar (if you use one), before heading out to the beach.

China Duran demonstrating good eating form.

In summer when the temperature is high, you might consider reducing the amount of practice time and increasing the number of sessions to comfortably maintain or improve your dog's level of skill. You may find it wise to work out in the early morning or late evening to take advantage of the cooler temperatures.

Talk to your veterinarian about how much food and water you should give your dog and when you should feed him. Most dogs enjoy playing Frisbee so much that they don't know when to stop, so you must be the one to exercise judgement and restraint. Wait at least two hours after doggie mealtime before serious exercise and don't feed or force fluids immediately after a workout. If he is really panting, give your dog only small amounts of water or ice cubes or he'll drink too much too quickly and get sick. Ideally, give him some time to cool off first.

Frisbee Familiarization

As I have said before, initial Frisbee training can begin when a dog reaches three months of age. I began training Wizard at this age by using a Frisbee as a food dish. Doing this made him feel comfortable around it. One word of caution: do not let your dog play with a Frisbee or use it for teething on his OWN. After your dog eats from it, put it away until the next meal or play session. There are plenty of other chew toys that you can give him. Your dog must learn that the Frisbee is only used for "special occasions." You don't want your dog to chew any disc laying around because it's expensive and could be catastrophic if, like me, you collect rare, irreplaceable Frisbees.

Tracking

Tracking is simply the ability to follow a moving object. With dogs, it's instinctive and natural, but it does take time to develop. An example of tracking in human development is a child's ability to catch. At first it looks like the child is closing his or her hands randomly and will never catch anything. With practice, his tracking improves and he can start to predict where a moving object will be for successful catches. A puppy not only has a short attention span, but no tracking skills. If you throw something over his head he will lose sight of it. Tracking takes time to learn and develop.

You can help your puppy's development by rolling a ball or favorite chew toy back and forth in front of him. You also might toss it up in the air a small distance and make sure that your dog follows the motion with his eyes.

Frisbees are a natural outlet for developing tracking and chase instincts. Wizard thinks that cats are also good for tracking. To him, cats are just Frisbees with fur and he always knows the exact whereabouts of our two.

Frisbee Basics

After introducing Wizard to the pleasures of eating dinner out of a Frisbee, I moved on to the next phase of his training: keep-away (not to be confused with tug-of-war). This was the way I chose to introduce the element of motion. First I moved (the empty Frisbee food dish) quickly, back and forth in front of his face and feet. Then I would slide the Frisbee upside-down across the floor a short distance to encourage his chasing instinct, remembering to always compliment him! Wizard would look at me horrified that I could throw away his food dish. He would dash after it to protect it. After a few days of this he felt less threatened, so I began to use a non-food Frisbee and thus it became a game to him. I continued with these exercises until he had the "play-time" idea and enjoyed the game. Whenever I referred to "the Frisbee" or "playing Frisbee" I would use a very animated, upbeat, happy tone; that way it seemed like a special game.

Naturally, if your dog chases the Frisbee and brings it back, give him lots of praise for being so smart. At first, it isn't important that any of these throws be far or fast, just that they're moving. In the early days, Wizard would usually chase my throw, occasionally grab it and rarely bring it back.

Some people suggest that you play tug-of-war using a Frisbee with your dog. I do not recommend this, because I feel that it encourages a "hard mouth"; a bad habit of chewing through the Frisbee. I agree that it's important to teach your dog to grab and jump, so instead, I recommend that you gently use a special play towel for your game of tug-of-war instead of a disc,

World Finalists Stan Sellers and Zulu.

and then only after your dog has his adult teeth.

Beware of a dog with a HARD mouth!

PHIL VAN TEE

Once your dog is comfortable with chasing and grabbing throws, it is important to teach him to bring the Frisbee back. A good way to get your dog to understand what you want him to do is to attach a long leash or laundry cord to his collar for a play session. After he makes a catch, call him. If there is any hesitation, just use the cord to gently pull him back while praising him for desirable behavior. Do this until your dog comes back on his own, but don't worry at this point if he doesn't bring the Frisbee back. Once your dog has mastered this lesson, try it off-leash. Repeat this frequently for short periods of time until he gets the idea. This exercise also can be done indoors.

If your dog comes to you without the Frisbee, you need to move to a small enclosed area to teach him retrieval. (Wizard started this way.) Get your dog really excited and then make a short throw. He will catch it and drop it without bringing it back and look expectantly at you. Tell him to get the Frisbee, then walk over to it and roll it. Eventually, he will most likely come over to it and pick it up and bring it a short distance to you.

Sometimes your dog may try to play a form of keep-away to get you to chase him for the Frisbee. NEVER play this game! Simply put his long leash back on and continue to practice until your dog comes when called. You must establish your dominance. Dogs are pack animals and in the wild there is always one leader. You must become your dog's leader. That is the only way he will consistently listen to you and do what you want. Naturally, you will be put to an occasional test, so be prepared to re-educate him if he has a "keep-away" relapse. For instance, after becoming proficient at Frisbee, your dog might suddenly get the urge to play keep-away instead of bringing it back. Don't ever let him get away with it! Get out the laundry cord, attach it to your dog's collar and work out with him until he remembers what is proper behavior. You'll be amazed how quickly he "remembers" his lessons.

Warm-Ups

I have rarely heard people speak about warming up their dog before exercising. In dog training you can't say, "give me five jumping jacks to begin." Still, I believe it's a good idea to start out slowly and not make your first throw too far or encourage your dog to jump too soon after commencing play. Start with some short throws and rollers. Next, hold the Frisbee over his head to get your dog to jump and stretch his leg muscles.

Catching

When training your dog to catch the Frisbee, there are a few requirements to keep in mind. First, to be successful you have to get your dog's excitement level up. Tease him with the Frisbee using the keep-away game, the roller and the upside-down slider. He must WANT the disc. Depending on how quickly your dog progresses, and if you started with a pup, he might be four to five months old before he starts catching. Starting with an adult dog can take minutes or months depending on prior training and desire.

After Wizard started going for rollers, I returned to the smaller Pocket Pro (three inch diameter Frisbee). I would kneel down in front of Wizard and get him very excited by waving it around his face and moving it from side to side. Then I'd flip it right at him. He instinctively tried to catch it, for which I really praised him. This continued until he actually caught one. He got a big hug for that before I let him continue with this game. If he missed a catch, I would quickly reach over and take it off the ground before he could get to it. That way, he had to CATCH it to touch it.

Once Wizard started to catch the Frisbee and knew that catching was the

Eldon McIntire with Hyper Hank and Amy Carter on the White House lawn.

Gary Suzuki and Sam performing at the Los Angeles County Fairgrounds.

game, I moved on and used several discs instead of one. I would flip them to him one at a time. When he began to get fairly proficient at this, I started to flip them to one side or the other. By doing this, I forced him to move to the disc. He would catch one and then look for the next. This accomplished a few goals: It gave him practice catching, it prompted him to think about moving to the disc and it got him used to working with multiple discs.

Next, I worked with Wizard on upside-down and short vertical throws. After that, I progressed to longer, more difficult ones. Once your dog can catch a particular kind of toss, try starting with him at your side. Throw a leading toss about three feet. Remember to allow the dog to maintain eye contact with the disc.

Finally, the way to get your dog to run, jump and catch is to hold the Frisbee above his head. Your dog will naturally jump up for it. The jump should be short and low at first—inches, not feet. Let your dog's first leaping catch be successful by letting him take the Frisbee out of your hand. At first the Frisbee can be angled downward, but after he masters this, keep the Frisbee level or parallel to the ground (giving your dog the same perspective of the disc that he would have if it were flying). The next step is to let go of the Frisbee as your dog jumps up for it. This makes him move with the disc to catch it. From there, move the Frisbee from side-to-side and have your dog follow it until you make a short, three-foot throw. Gradually increase the length of your throws as his expertise increases.

Another exercise that you might want to try is to take your dog along while you play Frisbee with a friend. Encourage him to run back and forth and try to intercept your throws. Make sure he gets one occasionally and give him plenty of praise. Remember, this is just to be used as a supplemental exercise, otherwise you could give your dog a bad habit of stealing other people's Frisbees and therefore becoming a thief.

Jumping

To make your dog a leaper, you must wait until he is physically mature and ready for the physical shock of jumping and landing. Six months is usually a good age to start. Hold the Frisbee higher than he can jump. Make sure that it's just high enough for him to reach and as soon as he can reach it at one height, continue to gradually increase the height. Remember to hold the Frisbee parallel to the ground. Don't tease him by overdoing this. Three good jumps before each throw is enough to develop leg strength and jumping ability.

Some dogs will wait for the Frisbee to come down rather than jump up for it. One way to work on this is to attach a Frisbee to a pole by string (like a fishing pole) so that you can swing it away from your body. Then you tell your dog to get the Frisbee. This way you can move and control the height of the Frisbee which forces your dog to leave the ground for it. Gradually increase the height of the disc in practice. Praise him when he leaves the ground; later use a word like "Jump" when he does it so that you can use the same word in practice to reinforce the process.

A good method for developing your dog's form was told to me by J.P. Rees. Have your dog jump through a Hula-Hoop. This will encourage your dog to pull his back feet up and in when he is airborn.

Four-time World Finalist Zach

1989 World Champions Jeff Perry and Gilbert demonstrate a front flip.

Advanced Frisbee Training

Once the basics are mastered, you will probably want to attempt some advanced tricks with your dog. Puppies should be ready for advanced tricks at 6 to 12 months of age.

"Over"

One of the most useful advanced tricks is one I call "Over." It is versatile and can be used in two combinations. First, it can lead your dog into another trick during a performance and second, it can be used as a basis to teach him a more advanced trick. Once your dog knows this command, you can have him jump over your leg, back, head, etc., depending on his leaping ability.

Start by kneeling and having your dog jump over the top of your outstretched thigh toward the Frisbee you are holding. By this time in your training your dog should be interested enough in going for the Frisbee as a treat (if not, use food the first few times). You may have to guide him over the first few times as you repeat the command "Over." Teaching this to your dog shouldn't be tough because he is just making a little jump. If you want to be creative, you can have him jump over in one direction and then back the other way.

If he circles around instead of jumping over you, try the following exercise. Put a leash on your dog and kneel facing a wall, tree or fence with your knee against it. Have your dog jump over your knee. The wall will prevent him from running around in front of you, while the leash will prevent him from going around behind you.

Once he can jump over your thigh, stand up and have him jump over your leg. From there all it takes is repetition. If you want your dog to jump over your

Peter Bloeme and Wizard demonstrate a forward "Over" the leg catch.

Reverse "Over": by Peter Bloeme and Wizard

back, you may have to get on your hands and knees the first few times and possibly elicit a friend's help in guiding your dog. Later, all you should have to do is bend over and command "Over."

This is a powerful trick, because if you use it as suggested, it is a real crowd pleaser. Having your dog jump over you and doing tricks around you is good for showmanship. However, a word of note for competitors: Since the Frisbee is not being thrown or caught, do not use it to excess in competition. It will not add to your score. Later, to really impress your friends and the judges, have your dog jump over you and flip the Frisbee to him simultaneously. For example, as your dog jumps over your outstretched leg, release the disc so that he catches it on the way over. This can be done in many ways and will add to your total score if completed successfully.

The two-handed move, demonstrated below by Glenn Medford and Brittany is a good example of a two-handed throw and the command "Over." You start in

Two-handed "Over": by Glenn Medford and Brittany

a kneeling position and, using the two-handed throw, flip the disc straight over your head (lowering your head just to be on the safe side), as your dog leaps over you either from in front or from behind to catch the disc.

"Take"

Although you will not directly receive credit in competition for this trick, "Take" is invaluable as an extremely versatile learning technique. Simply get your dog excited with the Frisbee and hold it out to him and say "Take." Once your dog will do this on command, you can hold the Frisbee over his head, say "Take" and he will jump up and grab it out of your hand.

Later on, this command can be used when you want your dog to take the Frisbee out of your mouth *(see photos page 76)*, from behind your head or over your leg.

Once your dog understands the command "Take," you can easily work it into some advanced tricks by combining it with "Over." For instance, position your dog to your side, kneel next to him with your opposite leg extended, hold the Frisbee over your knee and have him jump over it, taking the disc as he goes. This trick can be expanded so that you do it standing up with your leg outstretched. From this position you can toss the

Take: four-time World Finalists Tony Frediani and Duke demonstrate a good warm-up jump.

Advanced "Take": by 1989 World Champion Jeff Perry. Jeff ends his routine with an advanced "Take" by having Gilbert jump into his arms.

Mouth "Take": by Mike Miller and Pro

Frisbee instead of handing it to him *(see photo page 73)*. This can be done in either direction.

A word of caution for doing leg-over tricks: Always extend the leg that is closest to your dog. This affords you some bodily protection.

To reverse this trick, stand sideways to your dog with your right side toward him. As he runs behind you, bend down and lift your right leg to a horizontal position so that he will jump over it. With your right hand flip the Frisbee over your leg. This takes excellent timing on your part; unless you are extremely flexible, you can't twist around to see him take off *(see photos page 74)*.

Other advanced "Takes" include making a "hoop" with your arms (they don't have to touch) and having your dog jump through them and take the Frisbee out of your mouth. A hoop can be enlarged by holding Frisbees. If you hold them in one hand the hoop area becomes about nine inches larger than your arms by themselves and if you hold discs in both hands, 18 inches larger. This will be big

Peter Bloeme and Wizard demonstrate the "Catapult" continuing on facing page.

enough for almost any dog to jump through *(see photo to right)*.

Here are a few other tricks you can do employing the "Take" command:

- Put the Frisbee on your head and have him take it from there.
- Kneel and put your arm out from your side; then toss the Frisbee to him as he jumps over it.
- Start with your right leg out and do a scissors kick so that your dog jumps over your left leg.

"Give"/"Drop"

Now that we have covered the "Take" command, it's time to mention the equally important counterpart—the release command. Some dogs will drop the disc at your feet while others practically need to have it pried out of their mouths with a mechanical "Jaws of Life." Since you may not have access to such a spreader, it's easier if your dog learns early in life to let go of the disc on command.

Two Disc Hoop: Reese Blake and Tara demonstrate good "hoop" form.

To teach your dog to drop the Frisbee on command, have your dog sit five feet in front of you and kneel before him. Toss the Frisbee to him and let him catch it. Then say "Give" (or "Drop"). If he doesn't readily let go, pinch the sides of his mouth with your left hand while grasping the Frisbee firmly in your right

hand. This is usually a slightly uncomfortable position so your dog will let go of the Frisbee. Compliment him and repeat the same sequence until he drops the Frisbee on command.

Vaulting

Vaulting is a technique in which you have your dog jump off a part of your body such as your back or thigh to get extra height, thereby increasing the difficulty and showmanship of the trick.

The first vault to learn is the "Catapult." It involves having your dog jump up and off your thigh like a springboard and then into the air to catch the Frisbee *(see photos pages 76-77)*. I started teaching Wizard this one by kneeling, holding a Frisbee above my head and then having him jump over my thigh with the "Take" command.

You may need to use the technique I mentioned *(see page 73)* for teaching "Over" to prevent your dog from running around you. Get a chair and sit facing a wall (tree or fence) with your knees touching it and put a blanket in your lap for protection. Then, have your dog jump into your lap from left to right. Next, hold the Frisbee up over your lap so your dog has to jump off your lap to get it. Finally, toss the Frisbee up. By this time, your dog will not hesitate to use you as a ramp.

Once you have taught your dog all the basic components of this trick, use it in a performance: Start by positioning your dog to your left. Next, bend your left leg so that your left thigh is parallel to the ground and rest your left foot on the lower part of your right thigh. This will provide you with the support you need. You will look somewhat like a Flamingo at this point. As your dog begins his leap

Chest Vault: by 1990 World Champions Lou McCammon and Scooter

1990 World Finals Runners-up Chris Breit and Mattie

"Back" Vault: by two-time World Finalists Ron Ellis and Maggy

off your bent leg, toss the Frisbee up over your head with your right hand. When done correctly, this trick is a big crowd pleaser. You can easily use one trick for multiple purposes, for instance I frequently use the catapult to create an interesting ending for our routine. Wizard jumps from my thigh as usual, but instead of tossing the Frisbee, I catch him in my arms and bow.

You will find it easiest to teach (and later to perform), vaulting from a set position and distance. This will provide important consistency.

Other combinations of vaults include tossing the Frisbee in the air, and then bending over and having your dog jump off your back into the air to make the catch. Lou McCammon and Scooter perform a remarkable variation on this one in the form of a chest vault *(see photos page 78)*. A word of warning though for competitors who do these type of tricks: a neoprene (diving) vest underneath your T-shirt is a wise investment. I have also seen hunting vests, sweaters and sweat shirts used for protection. For the catapult you might consider a thigh wrap. Otherwise, your dog's claws will scratch your thigh, back and chest, even if their nails are clipped properly.

Cautions On Vaulting

It is important to be aware that vaulting is not required in competition. There are many tricks in a Frisbee dog's repertoire that can be used in place of vaults. Jeff Gabel with Casey and Jeff Perry with Gilbert are World Champion teams who do not do vaults due to their dogs' size, yet they have been very successful in competition.

Four-time World Finalist Mark Wood readies his diving vest prior to a demo.

Advanced Frisbee Training

Some dogs are just too big for vaulting. Generally speaking, once a dog reaches 50 pounds it is not a good idea to attempt vaults. Vaulting CAN be dangerous to your dog because he will be coming down from great heights and could land in stressful positions. Before beginning training make sure your dog is in excellent physical condition. After your dog knows how to vault, don't overdo it in practice since vaulting includes much jumping and jarring. A couple of successful vaults a week should be sufficient to keep you both sharp.

If you do have your dog vault,

Five-time World Finalist Donna Schoech and Charity demonstrate multiples from a difficult standing position.

make sure you practice in an area clear of any objects that your dog could land on. Some competitors like Ron Ellis and Mark Wood like to have their dogs vault, but do so from a low position so their dogs are reaching heights that are within their normal jumping range. Although any athletic endeavor can be dangerous, if you are going to vault, I prefer this method as it is safest for your dog.

Multiples

Current competition rules allow up to five Frisbees for a routine, otherwise known as multiple discs. The true definition of multiples is simply using two or more Frisbees at once with your dog. This can be done with several quick, short throws or long floating throws where your dog has time to catch one then run under another one and catch it. I use the command "Two," so that Wizard will

Vertical Multiples: by Peter Bloeme and Wizard. The Frisbees move so quickly that one is usually in the air while Wizard is catching another. Multiples can be a good change of pace.

run for the first, make the catch and then immediately look for the next one without looking back at me.

I am often asked how you get your dog to drop the first disc so he can catch another. This is usually not an issue for people who start out with multiple discs, but it can be for someone who has been using only one disc with his or her dog.

Here is a sure-fire method: Flip the Frisbee at him and after he catches it say "drop." Immediately throw the next disc and continue with up to five Frisbees. Your dog will usually catch on quickly.

Here is another variation on this trick: Have him at your side to begin. Tell him "Go," and throw two Frisbees, one right after the other, the first short and the second a little longer. The effect is that there are two Frisbees in the air simultaneously and your dog will go and catch one and then the other.

This can be a very impressive trick. The easiest way to teach it to your dog is to create a word for a Frisbee in flight ("another") and to say it to the dog just as he has made a catch on the first throw. Do this on short throws and then progressively work longer and longer. Three-time World Champions Bill Murphy and Bouncin' Boo used this to perfection. Murphy would have three Frisbees in the air while his dog ran from one side to the other catching them. The move is not without risk, though, for if your timing is off, your dog simply goes from one miss to another. Precise throwing and timing are essential for this trick.

Craig Brownell's dog Zeuss demonstrates that eight is definitely enough!

Multiple Disc Catches

In short throws, such as front or back flips, it is possible to release two discs at the same time so your dog catches both discs simultaneously.

1989 World Champion Jeff Perry uses this trick in his routine with a front flip, while three-time world finalists Bill Watters and Air Major do it differently. Watters flips two discs in the air simultaneously and his dog catches one while Watters spins around and catches the other. My method is using a two-handed throw over my head where I toss two discs simultaneously. As Wizard catches one disc, I tap, then catch the other.

Some dogs will even catch one right after another without dropping them.

Advanced Frisbee Training

The best known multiple disc catching canine was Zeuss owned by Craig Brownell whose record was nine in his mouth at once and listed in the *Guiness Book of World Records (see photos page 82 of eight at one time)!* I don't think that this can be taught but rather is instinctive on the dog's part.

Front Flip: Using a short vertical throw, Peter Bloeme makes a toss over Wizard's head. Wizard jumps after the "bad" throw, spins, makes the catch, and lands safely.

Front Flip and Back Flip

The front flip and back flip are variations of the same trick. The flips are identical, though the dog spins its body in different directions. I've simply given each variation a name to differentiate them. In the front flip you have the dog spinning to catch the disc to your left, while the back flip is when your dog spins to your right.

Some dogs will do this naturally on short throws one way or another, but to teach these tricks I've found it easiest to start by kneeling with your dog about four feet in front of you. Remember to use lots of praise and reassurance as you follow these steps:

- Toss the Frisbee vertically to your dog as he stands in front of you.
- Gradually raise your toss so that he now has to raise up off his front legs.
- Next, make what appears to be a bad throw over his head and slightly to the side.

Back Flip: Peter Bloeme uses the roller delivery to make a throw over Wizard's head. Wizard starts to leave the ground, spins, does the flip and makes the catch.

If you have him sufficiently excited, he will go for it instinctively. Make sure you spot for him, so that if he comes down poorly you can guide him. For the back flip I use the roller delivery but throw it over his head from the same position using the same progression. Once your dog is catching the front or back flips make sure you say, "Front" or "Back" before releasing the throw. He will soon learn to associate the word with the trick.

Tapping: Peter Bloeme tosses the disc to Wizard upside-down. Wizard bounces it back with his nose.

Tapping

Tapping (some players call this tipping) is an original trick I developed which had never been done before in canine competition. I borrowed the idea from human Frisbee competition where a person bounces the Frisbee with his or her feet, fingers, elbows, head, etc. Here is how it works: I place Wizard about five feet away and flip the Frisbee upside-down (or right-side up) to him over his head. Instead of encouraging him to catch it, I say "Tap," and he hits it back to me with his nose. The year after our world championship victory, I elaborated on this one and had him not only tap the Frisbee but catch his own tap. I used the sequence "Tap-Catch." After seeing this, Frisbee dog owners wanted me to reveal how I taught it. Some even tried to bribe my wife into disclosing it. Others made up all sorts of wild theories. About four years later, I finally saw another dog do this trick.

Since then, I have seen three people do this trick so I will reveal how I did it. It was surprisingly easy once I figured out how to give Wizard the idea. Until that time it had been incredibly frustrating using beach balls and balloons since Wizard popped both going for catches before I came up with a method that worked. Some people resorted to using muzzles and tying their dogs mouths shut. I felt what was needed to teach the idea was for the dog to feel free enough that he would go for the Frisbee but still be unable to catch it.

Here's how I did it: I sat Wizard about three feet in front of me as I held his collar with my left hand. I would then toss the Frisbee flat to him but over his head *(see photos on page 84)*. As Wizard raised up on his hind legs to catch it, I would prevent him from catching it with my left hand by pulling him under it. Whenever I did this I said the word "Tap." After about a week of this I could let him go for it by himself and he would tap the Frisbee.

Butterfly Throw: by Two-time World Finalist Ron Ellis and Maggy

Butterfly

As described in the throwing section *(see page 60)* the butterfly (also known as end-over-end or third world spin) is more easily thrown with the spin moving toward your dog than away for him. It is usually easy to teach your dog the basics of this catch. Have him sit in front of you from a distance of about five feet. Get him very excited, tell him "Catch" and flip the disc toward him. He may go for it, yet may look a bit perplexed since it is something new for him. After doing it a few times, he will pick it up.

The butterfly catch can be combined with multiples; simply have your dog catch several throws in succession. Like other tricks, this one can be expanded upon. Some competitors will combine this and the front or back flip. The thrower tosses a butterfly above the dog thereby causing him to do a flip to catch the Frisbee.

Props

With the exception of uniforms, props are not allowed in competition. However, they can still make for interesting demonstrations. The use of hoops, canes, etc. with a well-trained Frisbee dog can be entertaining and crowd-pleasing.

The next chapter discusses the "thrill of victory and the agony of defeat" while providing information on competing with your dog.

1990 World Finalists Tad Bowen and Z Weyand

Competition

The first major Frisbee dog contest was held in 1974 at California State University at Fullerton, with radio station KFLA and Wham-O as sponsors. It was called the "First Annual Fearless Fido Frisbee Fetching Fracas" (What a great name!). More than 100 canines entered. Ashley Whippet was considered a "ringer" (too professional) and was not allowed to compete. Two of Ashley's good friends, Eldon McIntire with Hyper Hank and Ken Gorman with Schatzie, took the top honors.

The next big canine Frisbee event was a series of demonstrations sponsored by Wham-O at the Rose Bowl at the 1974 World Frisbee Championships. Following that, the events were known as "Catch & Fetch" contests sponsored by Kal Kan.

From 1978 to 1989, Gaines Dog Foods maintained the sponsorship of the world championships for disc-catching athletes. In 1982, the tournament was re-named the Ashley Whippet Invitational in honor of the great Ashley Whippet who had become the epitome of the Frisbee dog. It may be Ashley Whippet's most important legacy. In 1990, the Carnation company's "Come 'N Get It" brand dog food took over the sponsorship.

Come 'N Get It invites all owners of accomplished canine athletes, as well as novices, to test their Frisbee-catching abilities in competition with their pets. The competitions are free and open to all dogs—purebred or mixed. Come 'N Get It supplies all materials to participating community parks, recreation departments and contestants.

In 1990, Come 'N Get It sponsored approximately 100 local contests and six regional finals which culminated in the World Finals, held on the Mall in front of the Smithsonian Air and Space Museum in Washington, D.C.

Three-time World Champions Bill Murphy and Bouncin' Boo

It is estimated that more than 300,000 dogs and their owners play Frisbee in parks, at beaches and in back yards. Not all people enter the world of competition, but in 1990 some 10,000 throughout the country did. Even if you don't plan to compete, I recommend going to a few contests with your dog. First, you'll get some idea of what the contest is all about. Second, I know it may seem unlikely, but I'm convinced that your dog will catch on, get excited and learn just from watching other dogs play. I took Wizard to all the contests I could and he ardently watched, learned and cheered (barked) the competing dogs on. Third, it's a good place to network with other dog owners and ask any questions you might have about training. Finally, you may see, or be inspired to create, a trick you hadn't thought of before. To find out the schedule and location of Frisbee dog tournaments in your area, contact Ashley Whippet Invitational (AWI) headquarters *(see Appendix)* and start sharing a wonderful experience with your pet.

Competitive Events

Since rules can change at any time, I would suggest that you contact the AWI headquarters *(see Appendix)* for the latest guidelines.

- **Basic Throw And Catch:** This is normally an introductory event on a field marked with a 34 yard diameter circle. The thrower starts and stays in the center of the circle and is allowed only one Frisbee. Although the thrower must throw from the center of the circle, he or she may leave the circle to retrieve the Frisbee if necessary. The dog/owner team gets 90 seconds to score as many points as they can. Throws outside the circle must be attempted but if the throw is caught within the circle, the team receives one point. If the dog catches a throw outside the circle but has any paw on the ground (OTG), two points are awarded. Finally, if the dog catches the Frisbee outside the circle with all paws in the air (ITA), he scores three points.

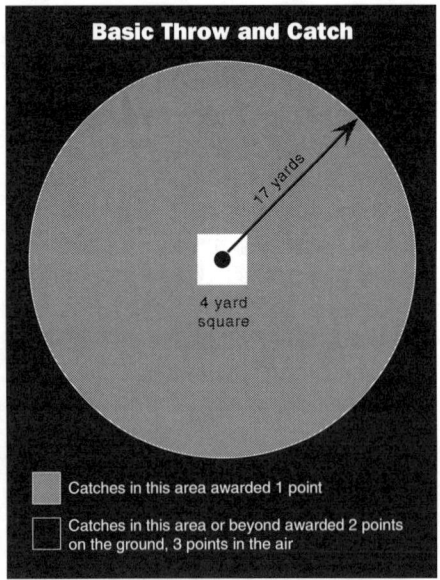

- **Mini-Distance:** This event tests both accuracy and strategy and it challenges the contestants to obtain as many points as possible for successful catches at various distances. The time allotted is one minute. The field is laid out similarly to a football field with yard markers. Using only one disc, the thrower must be behind the throwing line, but may cross the line to retrieve the Frisbee if necessary. For a team to score any points, the Frisbee must travel and be caught past the 20 yard marker. There are two

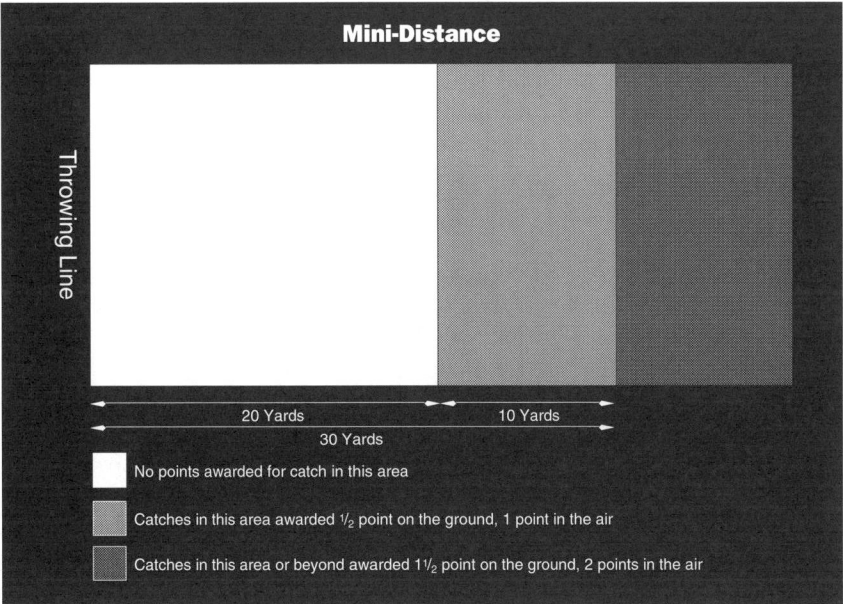

catching possibilities: on the ground (OTG) and in the air (ITA). If the dog completes a catch between the 20 and 30 yard marker he receives one-half point for OTG and one for ITA. A catch beyond the 30 yard marker scores one and one-half points for OTG and two points for ITA.

- **Freeflight:** Freeflight is exactly what the name implies. Here dog and owner have 90 seconds and up to five Frisbees to show their skills.

The following criteria are utlized by judges to score the freeflight round of the competitors (judged on an Olympic scale of 0-10) and taken from the 1991 official AWI guidelines for Freeflight performance:

Three-time World Champions Bill Murphy and Bouncin' Boo are skilled at Mini-Distance.

Degree Of Difficulty

"A demonstrated ability by dog and thrower to effectively perform attempted throws/catches of a non-routine nature with consistency. Including high-risk maneuvers, throws with varied spins, and catches where dog does not have eye contact with thrower and still succeeds; even where second or third effort is required."

Execution

"Consistent, smooth completion of maneuvers in a routine which emphasizes teamwork in the progression of throws and catches; particularly where they are of a non-routine nature. The judges look for quality here, not necessarily the number of catches made or not made."

Leaping Agility

"A consistency of throws and catches, with the disc in-flight, that showcase the dog's style and grace in motion. Note: The use of vaults, while highly entertaining and often spectacular, should be tempered with consideration for the animal's welfare. Excessive heights, or frequent repetitions of vaults, which employ the thrower's body as a launching pad, will not increase the possibility of a higher score."

Showmanship

"A demonstrated ability by the dog/owner team to perform unique, novel, or even trend-setting disc-in-flight maneuvers (starting or ending with the disc in

Agony and Ecstasy: World Finalists Bill Watters and Peter Carlos

flight) requiring a high degree of ingenuity, teamwork and consistency."

Local Competition

The local and state competitions are not prerequisites for entry to the regional event, nor is a previous minimum qualifying score required. Anyone may enter up to two dogs.

Participating cities (chosen by the sponsor), have the option of conducting either the "Freeflight" or the less sophisticated—and thus easier to judge—"Basic Throw and Catch." Sticking to this basic format is recommended because recreational officials who judge those contests may be unfamiliar with the intricacies of the sport. Come 'N Get It provides awards, T-shirts and Frisbees to competitors.

Three-time World Champion Alex Stein judging.

Regional And World Finals

Currently six regions in the U.S. are recognized: Northeast, South Central, Southeast, North Central, Southwest, and Northwest. The region you compete in will depend on the state in which you live. Since this information can change, I recommend that you contact the Ashley Whippet Invitational *(see Appendix)* for current policies.

At the regional finals, Come 'N Get It provides trained judges (such as Alex Stein, Eldon McIntire, Jeff Perry and myself), scorers and time-keepers, in addition to the awards, T-shirts and Frisbees. The competition consists of two rounds of freeflight and one of mini-distance. Sometimes, the top three dogs perform pre-game or during the halftime of a major sporting event. First and second-place finishers win an expense-paid trip to the world finals.

At this level of competition it is not uncommon to have the first, second and third-place winners finish within one point of one another. Some dogs excel at leaping ability and others at teamwork, so it's wise to develop your dog's all-around abilities to gain as many points as possible.

The Ashley Whippet Invitational World Championship winner receives a $1,000 U.S. Savings Bond, the runner-up receives a $500 U.S. Savings Bond and the 2nd runner-up, a $250 U.S. Savings Bond. All world finalists receive complete outfits, handsome trophies and usually local and national publicity.

Judging

As a national judge for canine competition for over eight years, I can honestly say that judging is a most thankless job. Not only is it extremely difficult, but because judging is somewhat subjective, competitors have a hard time in their own minds differentiating themselves from the competition.

Since judging is subjective by nature, and since it has no hard and fast rules, I will try to provide some insight, not only to help competitors understand how the judges come up with their scores, but also to help those who may judge.

- Degree of Difficulty is based on how advanced as well as how varied the tricks are. A team that does an incredible trick repeatedly will receive a lower score than one with a varied routine. An even routine is better than one with lots of highs and lows.
- Execution is based on the percentage of successful catches that a dog makes. Consideration is given to contestants who attempt many catches in their routine compared to those who are more cautious. Repetitive short multiple throws do not necessarily increase a competitor's score.
- Leaping Agility involves style and grace, as well as how high a dog leaps from the ground in proportion to its size. A large dog is generally going to jump higher than a small dog. This is taken into consideration. Leaping scores are not heavily weighed on vaults where the dog is getting assistance from the thrower. Leaping agility is judged on consistency, style and grace and not on one or two great leaps.
- Showmanship is the ability of the dog and thrower to work together as a team—smoothly and with confidence. Proper disc management is crucial to good showmanship. Competitors who dash madly to retrieve discs and appear haphazard in the manner in which they conduct their routines will likely receive low showmanship scores.

One way to score a routine is to divide a blank piece of paper up into three columns marked "A," "B" and "C." Every catch and miss is counted. An "A" catch is considered very difficult, a "B" catch is average, while a "C" catch is reserved for short simple catches. Mark an X for each catch and an O for each miss in the appropriate column. This will provide a method of reviewing and scoring each routine.

World Finalist Mattie demonstrating a hoop "Take" out of Chris Breit's mouth.

World Champions
1975: Alex Stein/Ashley Whippet
1976: Alex Stein/Ashley Whippet
1977: Alex Stein/Ashley Whippet
1978: Jim Strickler/Dink
1979: Jim Strickler/Dink
1980: Frank Allen/Kona
1981: Bob Cox/Belmond
1982: Bill Murphy/Bouncin' Boo
1983: Bill Murphy/Bouncin' Boo
1984: Peter Bloeme/Whirlin' Wizard
1985: Bill Murphy/Bouncin' Boo
1986: Chris Barbo/Kato
1987: Jeff Gabel/Casey
1988: Jeff Gabel/Casey
1989: Jeff Perry/Gilbert
1990: Lou McCammon/Scooter

Hall Of Famers
Peter Bloeme/Whirlin' Wizard
Jeff Gabel/Casey
Irv Lander
Eldon McIntire/Hyper Hank
Bill Murphy/Bouncin' Boo
Alex Stein/Ashley Whippet
Steve Willett

1981 World Champions Bob Cox and Belmond at the Rose Bowl

Contest Promotion
The Bethesda, Maryland-based advertising agency Earle Palmer Brown sent Irv Lander (Executive Director of the Ashley Whippet Invitational) some creative promotional advertisements for Frisbee dogs. I couldn't resist reprinting them here, with Irv's permission. They have won international acclaim and could well become classic posters:

- **See the only athletes who scratch themselves more than baseball players...**
  Come to this year's Dog-Frisbee Championship and you'll see some great throwing, running and catching. Not to mention some embarrassing sniffing, scratching and licking.
- **Imagine Michael Jordan with fur.**
  If you think Air Jordan can fly, wait until you catch Air Fido at this year's Dog-Frisbee Championship. We promise, it will beat anything you'll see in the NBA. By leaps and bounds.

- **Who will lick last year's champion?**
  This year's Dog-Frisbee Championship promises to be a real battle. So enter your dog today. Even if he doesn't beat last year's champ, we're sure he'll get in a few good licks.
- **See pets perform stupid human tricks.**
  At this year's Dog-Frisbee Championship you'll see man's best friend perform some of man's best tricks. They'll run. They'll jump. They'll catch.
- **They fly through the air with the greatest of fleas.**
  The acrobatics at this year's Dog-Frisbee Championship promise to be more daring than ever. So bring your dog. Bring your Frisbee. And get ready to watch the fur fly.
- **The most fun your dog's had since your leg.**
  If your dog's becoming too attached to you, bring him to this year's Dog-Frisbee Championship. After all, with all the exercise he's been getting, he might have a leg up on the competition.
- **Beating last year's champion could be a real bitch.**
  If you and Fifi think you're tough enough to topple last year's Dog-Frisbee Champion, give it a try. But just remember, it's going to take one tough mother to win. And all you have to do is sit. And stay.

Competitor makes dazzling leap at the Rose Bowl.

Three-time World Finalist Jendi Holmes and Scotland

Competition Tips

have competed successfully for 11 years in Frisbee tournaments on my own and more recently with Wizard. Along the way, I have developed some guidelines I feel will benefit anyone interested in competition.

Know The Rules

I know this one sounds extremely obvious, but many people don't read or understand the rules and then they suffer the consequences. Review the current guidelines available and make sure you understand all the rules, not only what is allowed but what is NOT allowed. If you have any questions, have them answered by the officials in charge before the contest begins. Sometimes you can profit by something that isn't specified in the rules. For example, in the 1984 Ashley Whippet Invitational World Finals, Wizard and I squeezed a few precious extra seconds into our routine. The rules stated that time would begin with my first throw (disc leaving my hand), so I choreographed our routine so the two of us did simultaneous moves before ever making a throw. This benefited us in both the teamwork and showmanship categories without taking away valuable competition time.

Be Creative

Explore various maneuvers that may (or may not) work. Try anything and use whatever works. I highly recommend that while you are trying new things, have someone videotape you and your dog. In review, you may find some moves you

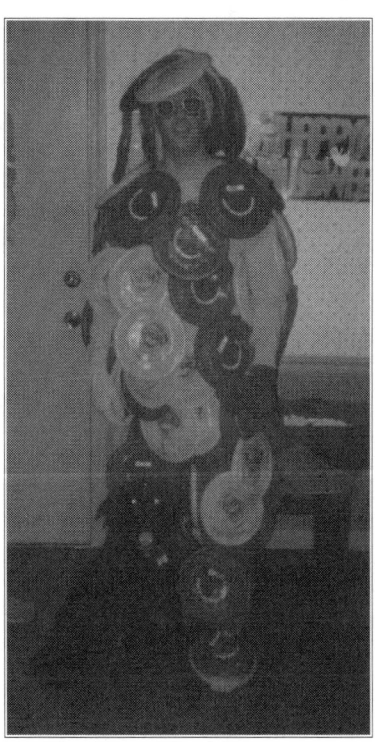

Four-time World Finalist Mark Wood in costume with Zach (who isn't).

thought looked great were not nearly as impressive as pictured in your mind's eye, but the reverse can also be true.

Practice All The Events
I have seen many competitors work only on freeflight and then lose a regional competition on the mini-distance round. There is no excuse for this. Remember, if you can lose a regional on mini-distance, you can just as easily win the competition on it.

Before you begin, count your Frisbees to make sure you have the correct amount, five or less. Once you and your dog go out to the competing area, give yourself a few seconds to relax. Take a couple of deep breaths and get in tune with your dog. Your success is a product of your mental attitude. Be upbeat!

Choreography
When I first started judging state, regional and world championships, I was surprised to find many of the best teams didn't have performances that made them look sharp consistently. I took advantage of my early observations as a judge by becoming the first person to choreograph an entire competitive routine. Keep these things in mind:
- Rehearsed choreography (this doesn't have to be elaborate) is now standard for competitors. This includes performing to music.
- Working out to the same song every time will make it easier to remember the correct sequence of moves so you don't leave something out.
- Remember to bring your musical recording with you to the competition.
- Make sure your tape is cued and marked properly (right side, wrong side, your name, your dog's name) for the sound man at the event.

Your dog doesn't have to know many different tricks in order for you to put together a perfectly acceptable routine. You DO need to discover how best to utilize your dog's particular skills. For example, if all your dog can do is run straight away from you and make a jumping catch, use some variety. Throw in one direction and then in another, then both short and long, and move around. If your dog knows two tricks, incorporate them by varying speed, timing and distance. Remember that you are being judged as a team and therefore you must look good both in form and uniform. Which leads us to...

Even dogs have egos.

Appearance/Costumes
You don't have to dress up like it's Halloween, yet your attire does

help to make an impression. At the 1984 Ashley Whippet Invitational World Finals, all contestants were issued uniforms for the competition, but they were only required to wear the sponsor's T-shirt. Some competitors actually chose to wear blue jeans. While the rules don't usually include a dress code, a coordinated appearance will add to your overall showmanship and work to your advantage. When I was competing I usually wore a color-coordinated, clean uniform featuring the sponsor's T-shirt, matching shorts, leg-warmers (popular at the time) and wrist bands and clean sneakers. Wizard was always freshly groomed, and wore his usual black and white fur coat adorned with "paw bands" that I designed for all four legs. Our goal (at the very least) was to project a professional image into the category of showmanship.

World Finalists Peter Carlos and Baxter demonstrate good fashion sense.

Strategy

My best advice is to HAVE ONE! Strategy is best defined as a combination of all the above. You should be alert, know the rules, choreograph to music if possible, practice, plan your clothing, be aware of weather conditions (especially the wind for throwing direction) and know the order in which you will be throwing. Make sure your music is clearly marked, cued and the correct side identified before turning it in. Be prepared!

Concentrate on what you and your dog are good at, but remember that the competition is a Frisbee-CATCHING event. Limit any tricks you do that include your dog taking the Frisbee directly out of your hand. While good for training, "hand-held" tricks (which were in fashion a few years back) are no longer worth the effort because they are not scored in competition. It doesn't matter if your dog jumps over your back, over your leg or twists in the air if all he is doing is taking the disc from you without a throw. On the other hand, if you flip the disc in the air first it will count as a catch and generate a score for you in all the categories.

Working With The Media

Since the sport of canine Frisbee is very media-oriented, there are some basic rules to keep in mind during both competitions and exhibitions:

Sponsor: The sport of canine Frisbee is wonderful, fun and exciting, but, it wouldn't exist without a sponsor. A sponsor is always looking for publicity; therefore, do your best to accommodate any media requests, as long as they don't interfere with your competition. Maintain a professional demeanor and be supportive of the sponsor in the quantity and quality of your comments.

Competition: While actually competing, do not let a cameraperson (still or video) control your actions. I learned this lesson when I was a junior champion. I did anything anyone with a camera wanted at the expense of my concentration. The media is looking for good footage and you are looking for a good score. Sometimes your agendas are the same; sometimes not. A cameraperson may ask you to perform before competitions, or between rounds. Since this can tire your dog and seriously affect your performance, you can tell the reporter politely that you will be happy to spend some time with them after the contest is over.

You also may find camera equipment or reporters in an area that interferes with your performance, or for some reason spooks your dog. I experienced this during the 1984 World Championships in Chicago. Wizard wouldn't return the Frisbee to me during the mini-distance round. Although the reason wasn't immediately apparent, I later realized that the camera crew behind us—complete with reporter, sound person, cameraperson and large tripod, had frightened him. Since a competition is geared to facilitate your best possible performance, you are within your rights to mention any concerns to the officials before you begin. They will understand and hopefully resolve the situation.

Exhibition: If you are working with a camera crew, find out what THEY want to shoot. Then help position them in a logical and safe area where they can get that footage. Explain what your dog is most likely to do as he gets warmed up or when he tires. Also mention that warming up, as in any sport, is necessary. Besides the concerns I mentioned above there are two additional points to keep in mind during an exhibition or private publicity session. Your first responsibility is your dog's SAFETY. This might mean positioning a camera crew a short distance away from the action. It might mean refusing to work on asphalt or in extreme heat. Finally, it might mean taking a BREAK to rest your dog. Cooperate, but keep your dog's best interest in mind.

General: Anytime you work with the media, always represent the sport and activity professionally. This means in your appearance and in your attitude. *(See Appearance, page 98 for more information.)* Be prompt, courteous and accommodating. It is acceptable to ask if you can have a copy of the photos or video shot, although this may not always be possible. Answer television questions in short, ten second "sound bites." Don't look straight into the camera and be sure to articulate. You will find that being a professional with the media (and your fellow competitors for that matter) will take you a lot further than being an egotist or showoff.

Travel

Travelling to my first world canine finals as a judge seem to foreshadow things to come for me as I exited from gate "K-9." Getting to events and demonstrations is typically done two ways: by car or by plane. It is important you familiarize your dog with both whenever possible, since travel can be stressful for you and your dog. There are many things to consider before hitting the road with Fido or Fifi.

Kennels And Crates

The first thing you should do is get a kennel (sometimes referred to as a crate) to serve as a travelling dog house. They can be purchased at a pet store or at the airport. I don't recommend you make the purchase immediately before a trip as you will need to get your dog acclimated with his mobile home to reduce the stress associated with travelling. Make sure that you clearly and permanently put your name, address and telephone number on the kennel. Do this immediately.

It is very important to buy the correct size kennel for your dog. Jeff Perry, the 1989 World Champion, called a manufacturer when he started travelling with his dog Gilbert and was told he should buy a kennel that did not allow his dog to stand up. This kind of misinformation is disturbing. The correct size is one that WILL allow your dog to stand up and turn around easily but not so big that he can be bounced all over. There are two types of kennels. One is very open and is used for the house, auto and

Here, 1990 World Champion Gilbert is firmly BOLTED into his modified kennel. The extra security became necessary because Gilbert did not take to a kennel easily. Before his owner's modifications, Gilbert escaped in Atlanta's Hartsfield Airport.

the outdoors while the other is made for air travel. The heavy-duty airline approved kennel needs to have adequate ventilation on the sides and ends. Make sure the container is "doggie-secure" to prevent your little Houdini from escaping at the most inopportune moments.

The books on dog training I recommend *(listed in the Appendix)* will teach you how to use a kennel in the home for training (such as housebreaking). Once your dog is generally comfortable with it, you can simulate the effect of flying by travelling with the kennel in the car. This can be done gradually until your dog feels secure in the kennel. This is also a lot safer than letting him run loose in the car, since an accident or short stop could cause your dog to go flying through the windshield, out an open window or out of the back of a pickup. I have always had Wizard lay down on the floor of the passenger side of my car when he isn't travelling in his kennel. You can also use your dog's kennel at home as a dog house.

When Alex Stein had several Whippets, he would stack all their kennels up (three high) and call them doggie condos. They loved it. When travelling, don't overload the kennel with a lot of junk. Do provide bedding and a couple of favorite toys (not Frisbees though). Also, don't feed your dog a few hours before driving, flying or, for that matter competing. It will only accentuate any likelihood of motion sickness.

Air Travel

When travelling by air it is best to arrange a "non-stop" flight to your destination. Next best is a "direct" flight, which means that you have one or more stops on your journey but there is not a change of planes. Finally, the worst type is the "connecting" flight. You not only have to make a stop in a city that is not your final destination, but you also have to change planes. This means your dog also has to change planes. On this type of flight there is a much greater potential for a mix-up. You could make the flight and your dog may not make the transfer or you both could miss the next flight due to a delay or your dog could be sent somewhere exotic. There are also commuter flights where the cargo area of the plane is too small for your dog. You may have to drive to a larger airport instead of having the airline decide the best route for you and your dog to take.

Make sure to let the airline know you will be travelling with a pet because usually you'll need to make a special reservation for him. There is a charge at the time of this writing of between $30 to $50 each way to fly your dog with you. Your dog's ticket can only be purchased at the airport or airline office; your travel agent cannot supply it. Still, you can purchase your dog's tickets in advance with your own ticket. I recommend that you buy a round-trip ticket for your dog. It is easier to go through the process just once for each trip. Due to various state regulations, to fly your dog you must have a travel certificate from your veterinarian that says that your dog is healthy, has the appropriate vaccinations and can travel safely.

If for some reason you can't travel on the same flight as your dog, he can be shipped as air cargo or freight. I have had to do this a few times due to conflicting, business-related travel. You need the same forms and kennel, but more cash. The crate is not considered excess baggage but rather as "freight," so you are charged by weight. You will need to go to the cargo/freight terminal of the specific airline your dog is flying. This terminal is usually found in more remote areas at airports. Make sure you check the flight times before you get to the airport so you can let them know when you want your dog to travel. Plan to arrive at least two hours before the flight. That will give the airline time to put your dog on the correct flight so you can have someone pick him up immediately on the other end. This kind of shipment is fairly common and the airlines are good about keeping the dog in a cool or heated room as appropriate. (Many thanks to various humane associations for bringing about such professional care.)

Air travel in the U.S. is pretty straight-forward compared to travel overseas. Some island countries, like England, require that you quarantine your dog for six months. Obviously, this would be difficult unless you were moving there permanently. Always check with the airline you will be travelling on for the most up-to-date information on the necessary credentials and certification.

When I flew to Berlin, Germany with Wizard for the NFL's American Bowl I went to the extent of getting German documentation for my veterinarian to fill out. Not one person checked our forms but you can bet they would have if we didn't have them. I found it interesting that coming back from Berlin, security X-rayed Wizard's kennel (without him in it).

Many dog owners have concerns and fears about flying with their pets so I will try to alleviate as many of those as I can. Since I travel extensively on Delta Air Lines, I contacted them for more specific information about travelling with a dog. They were also kind enough to give me a "backstage tour" of something Wizard knows quite well, in order to take the photographs used in this book.

We went to the airport that day and went through the whole process as if we were going on a trip. Wizard was confused because this time I went with him and he did everything but fly. I learned that there was a lot that I didn't know, despite being a frequent traveler. I want to thank Delta Air Lines for its help in providing this information.

The Flight Explained

Assemble your dog's kennel and make sure all bolts are tight before putting him in it. Make sure the kennel is marked with your name, address and telephone number in several places and check to see if the correct claim check is attached with the correct destination. Check your dog in at the ticket counter, or if you already have a ticket, at the curb.

Your dog begins his journey by entering security through baggage. He is then placed in a waiting area before being taken out to the plane. Pets are loaded last and taken off first, though they usually arrive at oversized baggage claim after the other baggage.

The area in the aircraft in which your dog travels is pressurized, heated and cooled as necessary, just like the plane's passenger cabin, but no meals or drinks are served and no frequent flyer points are awarded.

After arriving at your destination find out where oversize baggage arrives and wait there for your dog. If he doesn't show up right away, don't panic. Some airlines put the baggage out first and then bring out the dogs. I have waited as long as 45 minutes to have Wizard delivered to me. It is a good idea to let the airline personnel know you are expecting a dog. If there is no sign of him, go to the

When your dog gets checked in, make sure he gets the proper destination tags.

Next, your dog is transported by cart to a waiting area and then out to the plane.

At the plane, your dog will be put on a conveyor to the pressurized cargo area.

Here, Wizard is almost in the plane where his kennel will be stowed.

Baggage is placed around his kennel, without blocking the air flow.

Your dog will meet you at the oversized baggage claim area upon arrival.

airline office and report it. They will look on the plane and in the baggage area, and if there still is no sign of him, they will then put a trace on him for you.

Food And Water
When travelling, make sure you take along an adequate supply of dog food. Even if his favorite food is widely available, you don't want to have to go looking for it upon arriving after a long trip. I always bring enough food for an entire trip because it is easier than going out to find some. Because of the food, my luggage is generally heavier going out than it is coming home (which is usually advantageous for those like myself whose spouses love to shop 'til they drop).

Some people take along water from home for fear their dog's digestive systems may not be comfortable with local water. I have not found this to be a problem. Even in Berlin, Germany, Wizard, Ashley Jr. and Gilbert drank local water with no adverse affects. By the way, as I mentioned earlier, ice is sometimes better than water when your dog gets overheated. It gives your dog a chance to cool down slowly without becoming waterlogged.

Hotels
Most people assume that it is difficult to find a hotel that will accept dogs. This is simply not so, unless you are in the uncooperative state of North Carolina where it is against state law to have a dog in a hotel room. Otherwise, most Red Roof Inns, Holiday Inns, Marriotts and Howard Johnsons will accept your canine with you. However, this does not give you carte blanche to let your dog mess in the room or keep the neighbors awake by barking. As a responsible pet owner you have trained your dog to be obedient and, as such, should act and be treated accordingly. You may get some strange looks from time to time from people who are not as well informed. When checking in, immediately put the "do not disturb" sign on the door to prevent people from barging in on your dog and possibly freaking out. For your protection, when booking a room at a large chain ask the hotel or main reservation number whether your dog is allowed in that specific location.

There were a few times I had to sneak my dog into a room against the hotel or state's wishes. Once, I was doing shows in Pennsylvania and the weather was awful. I had to stop driving and find a hotel. There were none in the immediate vicinity that allowed dogs, and the temperature was below zero so I couldn't leave Wizard in the car. I thought I would be able to sneak him in the rear entrance until I noticed that the hotel had video cameras on all the entrances. With no other option, I had to take extreme measures. I stuffed him into a large, hard-sided suitcase and carried him into the room. The next morning it was considerably more difficult coaxing him into my suitcase, but "sometimes you have to break the rules."

1990 World Finals Runner-up Bill Watters and Air Major

Collecting Discs

Several years after I had started competing, I came across an unusual hobby: I found many competitors collecting flying discs. Quite a few of them had 50 to 100 discs (some many more) hanging on their walls, stuffed in boxes and strewn all over. I thought this was a pretty stupid practice—at first.

I actually became a collector unintentionally. I would get a tournament model here and there, then I would pick one up because it had a pretty logo. I started hanging them up neatly on the wall. Without knowing it, I had become an accumulator, or rather, a collector. Before I realized it I owned over 50 discs. For a year after that, I went wild and bought, traded and acquired anything that was flat, round and could fly.

At that point, I ran out of wall space, so I designed and built special shelves to hold my favorite discs vertically—like record albums. This way, I could display more discs per foot of wall space. I put the rest into storage. As with all collectors, I eventually reached a saturation point where I had to choose a specialty (limiting myself to one color, model, size, type, etc.) I chose to

Four-time World Finalist Gary Gomes and Kelly

Year: 1976
Color: yellow
Imprint: red

Year: 1977
Color: yellow
Imprint: black

Year: 1978
Color: white
Imprint: blue

Year: 1979
Color: white
Imprint: orange and black

Year: 1980
Color: white
Imprint: orange

Year: 1981
Color: white
Imprint: orange and black

Year: 1982
Color: clear
Imprint: red and gold

Year: 1983
Color: red
Imprint: gold and white

Year: 1984
Color: white
Imprint: blue

Year: 1985
Color: yellow
Imprint: blue

Year: 1986
Color: red
Imprint: blue and white

Year: 1987
Color: yellow
Imprint: blue and red

Year: 1988
Color: yellow
Imprint: blue and red

Year: 1989
Color: yellow
Imprint: blue and red
(northwest region only)

Year: 1989
Color: white
Imprint: red and black
(far west region only)

Year: 1989
Color: yellow
Imprint: blue and red

Year: 1990
Color: white
Imprint: blue and red

Year: 1991
Color: white
Imprint: blue

concentrate on Wham-O Frisbee discs (mainly Professional Models), plus the unusual. Some of my unusual discs are made out of cloth, some make sounds when thrown, some light up (not just glow), and some have strings attached so they return to the thrower. My collection now numbers in the thousands.

I'm sure collectors of all things share the same dream I had—that of accidentally stumbling across an amazing trove of whatever it is they collect. I dreamed about walking into an old toy store and while digging around in the back finding some antique discs hidden away in an old, dirty, dusty box. For me, this dream actually happened. However, it wasn't an old toy store but a new gas station.

While driving all night on a demonstration tour, I pulled into a brightly lit, modern Shell gas station at 2 o'clock in the morning. I pumped my gas and went inside to pay. I walked groggily to the counter. As I got there, it dawned on me there was something unusual about the colored plastic hubcaps I had observed on top of the cigarette machine. Upon closer inspection, I discovered they were "Unique U-1s," antique discs I had never seen or heard of. Despite my excitement I managed to casually ask the man at the counter where on earth he had found those old discs. He told me they had been sitting around his old gas station for years and he had just moved them to the new station to get rid of them! After negotiating a discount for "taking them all off his hands," I bought them for an undisclosed sum.

Why would a normal, reasonably intelligent person choose to collect discs? Because discs can be pretty, colorful, interesting, unique, historic and certainly conversation pieces. More importantly, they usually represent experiences and memories of the sport and a fun time in life.

Unfortunately, from a canine Frisbee collector's standpoint, there were some years where no year was imprinted on the discs used in competition. This has created some confusion in the canine disc collecting community. Therefore, I have pictured on pages 108-109 all the Fastback Frisbees that have been used in national competition.

If concealed Frisbees were illegal, Larry Taylor would be in jail (for hiding them from Angel).

Wizard's Competitive Experience

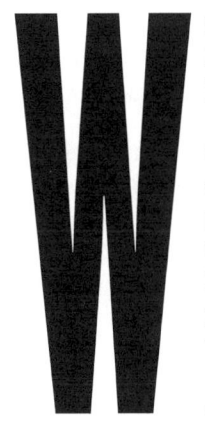

Wizard's first tournament was in 1984 at the Ashley Whippet Invitational (AWI) Regional in Boston, Massachusetts. He was just a little over one-year-old at the time.

I had been working in the Boston area the week preceding the tournament and it rained every day. Saturday June 2, the day of the contest, was no exception. When I woke up it was pouring as I headed out to see what the situation was at the tournament site. When I arrived, I saw Executive Director Irv Lander and Chief Judge Alex Stein waiting patiently in a parked car at the site. They said that due to the inclement weather the competition was postponed until Sunday.

Sunday surprised everyone by being a beautiful day—sunny and clear. I arrived early before anyone else and warmed up with Wizard. The next people to appear were the park department personnel accompanied by Lander and Stein.

Nancy Mullen of the *Christian Science Monitor* wrote on November 20, 1984:

"The stands are bristling with a lively mix of fans. A dozen athletes of various stripe and spot sit panting in anticipation. From his perch on the top bleacher, a miniature dachshund yaps out his impatience.

"The Ashley Whippet Invitational is about to begin.

"Gathered here on the Boston Common are dogs from all over the region who will vie for the title of champion canine Frisbee-catcher. To win, a dog must jump higher, run faster and catch more flying discs than any other contestant

Peter Bloeme with Wizard doing a backflip.

(allowing for differences in potential among the breeds). And he or she must do it all quickly, with style, grace and showmanship. In each of three rounds, the dog/owner teams will have only 45 to 90 seconds to show the judges their stuff.

"Out on the field, a little black and white border collie named Wizard is eying the plastic disc in his master's hand. 'Ready, Wiz? You're gonna JUMP,' the young man commands. Wizard's eyes flash and every muscle is a quiver. He's obviously ready. With a flick of the man's wrist, the disc goes soaring and the dog hurls himself after it like a bean out of a slingshot. For a brief moment, dog and disc float six feet above the ground. Then, with a half-somersault in midair, the collie grabs the saucer, hits the ground running and races back to his owner. After a quick pat and 'Good catch, Wiz,' he's off and flying again. Back in the stands, the fans—both human and canine—are exuberant. A black and white pooch named Erin is barking and leaping up and down in frenzied imitation of the action going on out in the field, while the toy dachshund makes his own observations on the proceedings."

The tournament was essentially a two-dog race between Wizard and a mixed breed named Isis. Mike Smith, owner of Isis and 1982 World Finalist, always impressed me with his vaults and consistency. In fact, Smith demonstrated to me early on in my experiences with Frisbee dogs that only your imagination limited the tricks that you could perform with your canine. To me that was quite an inspiration. Anyway, both our dogs scored the same in distance. When freeflight came, Wizard and I performed well enough to win. The competition was a tremendous learning experience for me. It is very different to practice and to perform than to compete. Winning made Wizard and I the Northeast Regional Champions and earned us the invitation to go to the world championships in Chicago that September.

World Finalists Mike Smith and Isis provided the author inspiration.

Preparing for the world championships was one of the hardest things I have ever done. Wizard and I practiced intensely the month before the tournament. My long-time friend Jackie Bernard helped in practice by timing and videotaping us. Afterwards we would critique the routine on video. I really benefited from being able to watch the routine from a different perspective. Things I thought looked good really didn't and vice versa.

By the time we left for Chicago, I felt Wizard and I were well prepared. Wizard and I would begin side-by-side about four feet apart and then simultaneously sit, lie down and roll over twice before starting the throwing and catching segment. I planned short and long throws with the disc right side up, upside down and vertical. In addition, Wizard would do multiples (more than one disc), execute back flips, tap/hit the Frisbee back to me with his nose (first time ever to be seen in public) and jump over my leg and back. I wore a designer top with red shorts, new sneakers and red wrist bands. Wizard wore a red bandanna with red paw (wrist) bands, a Peter Bloeme original. Finally, for music, I selected a song from the movie "The Wiz" to accompany our routine, with "Ghostbusters" as a backup.

The following article by Paul Sullivan was published in the September 7, 1984 *Chicago Tribune:*

"Besides the now-standard doggie backflips, spectators can expect some original moves never yet seen in the annals of disc-catching dogs.

"'We've got quite a few tricks in store,' countered Peter Bloeme of Brooklyn, a former World Frisbee Champ, who, with his dog 'Wizard,' is attempting to become the first pair of human/animal Frisbee champs. 'I'm not at liberty to mention any of them now. It's a dog-eat-dog world, you know.'"

After a long and uneventful drive from New York City, we arrived in Chicago a day early so Wizard could get used to the site and climate conditions, the most serious of which turned out to be the unpredictable, gusty, 20-mile-per-hour winds! Once we arrived, I had new cause for concern: Wizard had developed diarrhea, and I was afraid it would weaken him. I found it hard to eat and sleep because of my anxiety over Wizard.

The tournament was to take place over the course of two days. The first round of freeflight and mini-distance was scheduled for the morning and the second round of freeflight for the evening of the first day. The top five dogs would advance to the finals which were to be held the following day at Comiskey Park, home of the Chicago White Sox.

Peter Bloeme and Wizard demonstrate a reverse roller.

Day one, Friday, dawned clear, hot and windy. Not surprisingly, there were few spectators, as it was a business day. I felt our first round was a little shaky. Near the end of our routine, I made a throw that Wizard tipped (brushed) and caught. On the way back he suddenly stopped to smell the ground—he had never done that before. I ran over to him and tried to finish the routine with a flourish, but time had run out.

The next event was mini-distance. I knew that this event

could very well decide the outcome of the competition. The site was laid out so that we could throw in either of two directions. Because of the gusty winds, I spent a lot of time practicing to try and figure out the best direction in which to throw. I decided to go from the far end into the wind. We began and Wiz made a good first catch, but instead of bringing it all the way back to me, he stopped about 20 feet away. I didn't realize it at the time, but a camera crew behind me spooked him. Anyway, I went out, got the Frisbee, ran back and threw. Because of this delay I rushed, making a bad throw that Wizard couldn't catch. Since we only had 60 seconds total, I told myself to slow down and concentrate. I did, and my throws improved. Wizard was able to make two more catches, and compared to what the other dogs had done up to that point, this was excellent.

The scoring totals announced after that round included freeflight and mini-distance. Wizard and I were in second place, three and a half points behind the first-place team, Gary Gomes and Kelly, but ahead of the two-time world champions, Bill Murphy and Bouncin' Boo. I went back to the hotel and critiqued the contest on video while Wizard cooled down and rested in the air-conditioned room.

The second round of freeflight took place that evening, and was well attended. I had changed our music from the "Wiz" to the very popular "Ghostbusters" hoping to involve the audience. The crowd not only loved the music, but they loved our routine, too. We hit everything, had no breaks and finished with Wizard catching a long distance throw. We couldn't have done any better given the windy weather conditions and I was quite pleased. The contest was now in the hands of the judges. Gomes, who had been in the lead with Kelly, had as rough of a routine as I had in the first round. Yet, I was prepared for anything, because judging can be so subjective. As the cumulative scores were announced in reverse order from last to first, I held my breath. When I heard everyone else's name but mine, I knew we had caught up. In fact, we were in the lead by a quarter of a point. There was only one final round of freeflight to go and the two dogs, Wizard and Kelly, were starting in a virtual tie.

A forecasted change in the weather was of some concern to me: There was a chance of rain the next day, in which case the finals would be cancelled. If this happened, then the current first-place team would be declared the winner. In other words, Wizard and I would be the winners because we were in a quarter of a point lead. Although I didn't want to win that way, that night I was finally able to relax. I ate a leisurely dinner and then watched the video of the semi-finals to get psyched for the next day's competition, if indeed, there was going to be one.

For the first time all week I felt calm and had just settled down to bed when the phone rang. It was Alex Stein calling to ask if I would be awake for a few minutes because he wanted to talk. I invited him to come over. My first thought was that there was a mistake in the scoring and I prepared myself for the worst. After 15 minutes had gone by and Stein had not yet arrived, I went to look for him and instead ran into Irv Lander, who asked me if I had gotten the message about a meeting. I told him I hadn't but that Stein had just called me. He told me the officials needed to talk to me in Steve Willett's room (the sponsor's representative). Once there they informed me there had been a mistake in the scoring and instead of my being ahead, I was actually BEHIND by a quarter of a point. On the one hand, I was relieved it was nothing worse, but since I was now officially in second place, I started to get nervous. The first thing I did when I got back to the room was call for the latest weather forecast; suddenly it really mattered.

After hardly sleeping a wink, I woke to a dark and dreary day. It wasn't raining but looked as if it could at any time. The finals were to take place right before the White Sox game. When we arrived at Comiskey Park, it had gotten a little brighter but was still threatening.

Out of five teams, Wizard and I were set to go fourth, right after Bill Murphy and Bouncin' Boo, who, were now in third place. I was glad that we didn't have to perform first or last.

Our turn came and the wind had still not let up; it was swirling at an unsteady 20 miles-per-hour, but luckily the rain was holding off. Wizard started out strong. He hit all the difficult moves, giving me confidence, and we continued to do well. Television and media professionals were on the field during all the routines. They lined up behind second and third base in the outfield. Most of our routine had taken place in left field. When I heard the timekeeper call out "ten seconds remaining," I pointed toward home plate and told Wizard, "Go" so that we could finish with what I hoped would be a spectacular long distance throw and catch. Immediately after doing so, I realized that we had been told to stay off the infield, so with hand-signals I redirected Wiz around the media crews to right field. Wizard must have run about 100 yards before catching my 70-yard throw!

It was a great feeling to look up at the large "Diamond Vision" screen and see Wizard and myself 10 times larger than life. No matter what the outcome I was proud of Wizard. Despite his illness, the unfamiliar surroundings and all the attention, he had performed admirably. The final scores were announced. We had received a perfect "10" in each of the three rounds of freeflight for teamwork and one "10" for difficulty. Not only had I realized my dream of raising and training a world Frisbee dog champion, but I had done it on my first attempt; this was Wizard's first year of competition and now he was the youngest world champion ever.

Peter Bloeme and Wizard competing in the 1984 World Finals at Comiskey Park.

One hour after the competition ended the skies opened up and it POURED!

Nancy Mullen of the *Christian Science Monitor* wrote on November 20, 1984:

"At its best, the sport involves a subtle and highly developed interaction between dog and owner. With an impressive routine of hand signals, coordinated moves and precision timing, Peter Bloeme and his dog Wizard won this year's world final of the invitational 'paws' down."

And the *Boston Globe* on September 10, 1984, wrote:

"Leaping lizard, it's Wizard!

"Wizard the wonder dog knows when to quit—he's giving up competitive Frisbee-catching while he's ahead.

"But Wizard and owner Peter Bloeme of New York City went out in style, taking the $1,000 top honors at the Gaines Ashley Whippet Invitational Frisbee-catching tournament Saturday. That, says Bloeme, is nothing to bark at.

Peter Bloeme and Wizard winning the 1984 World Championships in Comisky Park.

"Bloeme, 27, who, himself, tosses the plastic disc toy professionally, has been training and preparing 2-year-old Wizard to be top dog since the border collie was a 4-month-old ball of black and white fur."

Based on my participation in the canine world finals as both competitor and judge, I can honestly say that The Ashley Whippet Invitational is the PREMIER Frisbee dog event. All expenses (food, travel and lodging and uniforms, including shirts, shorts, socks, Frisbees, carrying bags and beautiful jackets) are paid. To top off the event a wonderful awards banquet is held. For a competitor who reaches the world finals, no matter how he or she finishes, it is a great achievement and a lifelong memory.

Professional Appearances

As a result of each of our world championship titles, Wizard and I have had many exciting opportunities come our way, both separately and together. These have included television appearances on *"Late Night with David Letterman,"* Cable News Network (CNN), *"Good Morning America,"* George Michaels' *"Sports Machine,"* Steve Allen's *"The Start of Something Big,"* PBS' *"Cats & Dogs,"* *"Live with Regis and Kathie Lee,"* *"CBS Youth Invitational: Frisbee"* and ESPN. We've also been featured in articles in *USA Today, New York Post, Christian Science Monitor, Sports Illustrated, Dog World* and *Dog Fancy* along with a host of others. Wizard was even part of the beginning of the Disney movie, *Flight of the Navigator.*

Many years ago, not long after I won the Men's World Frisbee Championships in 1976, I was invited to appear on the nationally televised game show *"To Tell the Truth."* As you probably know, each show featured someone who had a unique accomplishment, along with two "impostors" claiming to be that person. The three guests would appear on stage in front of the show's host and a panel of four celebrities. After the announcer read a mini-biography of the guest, the panel would have to figure out through questions and answers who was telling the truth—thus the show's name. During my performance I stumped the panel!

At first I had mixed feelings about being on this particular show because as a 10-year-old I had been watching it when I was told that my father had passed on. However, by appearing on television on that show, I had somehow

Co-hosts Peter Bloeme and Tom Brookshire during taping of the "CBS Youth Invitational: Frisbee" at Six Flags Over Georgia.

reconnected with my father because I knew how proud he would have been to see me there. And as a youngster, I never dreamed that someday I would be in that category of "unique" people. So much had happened to put me there.

Part of the fun of what I do entails using my expertise in an advisory capacity. Not long after *"To Tell The Truth"* I was selected to be the co-host and technical adviser for a 30-minute CBS television special called *"CBS Youth Invitational: Frisbee."*

My next TV appearance was on *"Challenge of the Sexes,"* a popular celebrity-type television game show featuring prominent men and women athletes competing against one another. As the current Men's World Frisbee Champion I competed against Monika Lou, the 1976 Women's World Frisbee Champion. I narrowly edged out Lou for the win.

Peter Bloeme with Vin Scully during "Challenge of the Sexes."

Throughout my professional career I had appeared on many local and national television shows. Yet, there were two that I really wanted to do: *"The Johnny Carson Show"* and *"Late Night with David Letterman,"* both on the NBC network. My opportunity finally arose about a year after Wizard won his world title.

Quaker Oats' publicity department told me that Alex Stein had appeared with Ashley Whippet on *"Late Night with David Letterman"* a couple of years earlier and that the Letterman producers hadn't been pleased with the segment due to Ashley's inability to perform "on stage" in the studio. Ashley's abilities and training did not allow him to perform his type of tricks indoors in a small studio. He was a spectacular outdoor performer who needed a large amount of space. Stein tried to explain this to them before shooting, but they wouldn't listen. He even suggested that they go outside and film something for the show. The result was that the Letterman people weren't keen on having another Frisbee dog on their show.

"Look, Mr. Bloeme," the producer told me, "we've already had a Frisbee dog on our show and to tell you the truth, he just didn't work out very well. We're sure Wizard, here, is a fine performer, but, with the confines of the studio and all, I'm sure you understand."

"I understand," I said. "Ashley Whippet was a great outdoor performer, but he couldn't do tricks very well indoors. I've trained Wizard to work in small areas. I'm sure if you see some film clips of Wiz, you'll see he CAN perform indoors."

"Fine, kid. We'll take a look."

Not long after viewing the tapes of Wizard, the producer called, saying he wanted to see Wizard and me at the studio for an audition. I was thrilled. Wizard wagged his tail. Now, at least we had a chance.

After varied and assorted arrangements, a time and date were set. When we arrived, I noticed a narrow, three-foot red carpet on the floor in the studio. Although I didn't know why it was there I used it to warm-up Wizard while I waited for the producer, director and some other production people to appear. When they did, my show expertise came out: I performed one of my school shows which included all of Wizard's tricks. Since I trained him with the idea of working in the confines of small areas, he did great.

"Peter, he's wonderful. I must admit, we really didn't think it would work out," the producer said after we had finished our audition. The rest of the production crew echoed their accolades. The only ones on stage who weren't excited and pleased were the stage crew because it turns out, we were using their carpet. Little did they know we would be back.

"Well, Peter, Wizard," the producer said, patting Wiz's head, "we really liked you both. We will be in touch." After they were out of earshot, I sighed, saying to

Peter Bloeme and Wizard on "Late Night with David Letterman."

Wizard, "At least we got a tryout and did our best, so we couldn't ask for more."

That night the phone rang. It was the Letterman show. I crossed my fingers.

"Mr. Bloeme," the producer said.

"Yes?"

"We would like to know if you and your dog are free to do the Letterman show tomorrow night. We had originally hoped New York Yankee's owner George Steinbrenner could do the show, but because of the possibility of the baseball strike, he can't appear. Could you make it?"

"I'd be thrilled to do the show—tomorrow or any day," I said. The timing couldn't have been better because due to their vacation schedule, the show was being taped to be shown two weeks later. That way, I could "wake the kids and phone the neighbors" and let everyone and anyone know about the show in time to tune in.

The show was thrilling for me. Wizard and I were treated first class: They gave us our own dressing room. They had me wear stage makeup. We could have any non-alcoholic drink we wanted. I chose Perrier with a twist of lime. Wizard chose plain water.

Naturally, I was extremely nervous before going on. I mean, it WAS national television and all that. But at the same time I was terribly excited.

Letterman began announcing the show's line-up and got to me, "And a man who has brought us a dog, his name is Peter…(look of puzzlement) pronounce it for me Kevin…[he asked offstage]…Peter Bloeme [correctly pronouncing it Blerm]. Make a guess how this man spells his name. But you know he has brought an amazing, wonderful, sweet dog who's going to do some unbelievable things for us, that will be Peter Bloeme. And if we have time we will get into his last name a little bit later. Can I show them the last name…[gets the cue card and shows card]. Now here is Peter…now say that quietly to yourselves at home…"

Then he did a skit with the NBC Bookmobile. The routine was going slowly so Letterman said, "Mr. Bloeme is here tonight."

"Very exciting," the librarian lady replied.

It continued to go slowly.

"Maybe it's time to bring out Mr. Bloeme," quipped Letterman.

There were three guests on the show that night and I was the second, after Dr. Ruth Westheimer, the famous sex therapist and psychologist.

The diminutive Westheimer was talking about her new sex game in her unmistakable accent.

Letterman interrupted, "Let me ask you something. Does the word Bloeme appear anywhere in the…"

Westheimer replied, "No but it just may…I'll tell you why I did this…"

"Very nice man, got a great dog too, really sweet dog," Letterman continued.

"Let's talk about sex not dogs," Westheimer said a little testily.

After a commercial break Wiz and I ran out on stage. The studio audience had been treated to a song by the band, which was excellent, but very loud. Since I was already nervous back stage, I wondered if their playing would affect Wizard.

When Letterman introduced us, we came out as though we were at a professional sporting event.

Letterman, a consummate dog lover, kept petting Wizard and saying what a beautiful animal he was.

"Now, then, what are you going to have Wizard do?"

He really seemed to enjoy Wizard's performance. It's tough working indoors on a small carpet, but we managed to get in many interesting tricks. The catapult was by far his best. The camera man had missed it and my friends in the studio audience told me later on they had seen him wince in disappointment.

We ended with Wizard taking the Frisbee out of Letterman's mouth, at least, that's what was supposed to have happened. Letterman put it in his mouth and then quickly took it out complaining that it tasted like Gaines Burgers which got a big laugh. Then, in spite of my warnings, Letterman didn't let go of the Frisbee in time, so it was more of a collision. He may very well have planned it that way. It looked great on instant replay.

Letterman was wonderful to work with. He truly enjoyed Wizard and the segment. What may surprise people about appearing on a show like Letterman is that he doesn't meet with the guests before the taping. The producer told me that is because he wants the exchange with the guests to be fresh. After the show, Letterman came over to us, and shook my hand and Wizard's paw.

"Peter, Wiz," he said, patting Wiz's head, "very impressive showing. He's a great dog."

My only regret was not having a chance to ask David what his top ten things to do with a used dog disc were.

Many of the films I've appeared in were never released to the general public because they were "industrials," private films used for industries or companies. One of the most interesting industrial film projects I participated in was *"Sea Dream,"* a three-dimensional film for Marineland in St. Augustine, Florida.

It all started innocently enough. "Mr. Bloeme?" a voice on the other end of my phone asked hesitantly, having difficulty, as usual, pronouncing my name. "My name is Murray Lerner. I'm a film producer and director and I'm looking for someone who can throw a Frisbee. Wham-O told me you're the man for me. Do you think you're accurate enough to throw a Frisbee directly at a camera for some special effects in a film I'm doing?"

Peter Bloeme and Wizard with Steve Allen during taping of the show, "The Start of Something Big."

"What? Was he kidding?," I asked myself.

"Mr. Lerner, I am the world accuracy champion and a Frisbee professional. If a disc can be thrown accurately at a camera, I can do it," I replied as modestly as possible.

The filming took place on Marineland's beach in St. Augustine, Florida. Once the shot was set up, it dawned on me why Lerner had to have someone extremely accurate. He wanted a Frisbee thrown directly at the camera to invoke the full 3-D effect. To protect his equipment, he had a large Plexiglass sheet set up in front of it. All I had to do, from 20 yards away on a windy beach, was to throw and hit a spot three inches high by six inches wide. To make matters even more difficult, he was filming in slow motion. That meant I'd have three tries for every large reel of film. Filming in slow motion requires the film to travel faster than normal through the camera. Each miss would add to the cost of the filming and compound the pressure on me. To save on film, I practiced a lot and each time I thought I was doing well, Lerner would tell me to throw closer to the center of the lens! By noon he felt we had some good "takes in the can" (film talk for film already shot), so we went on to some easier beach scenes.

The next day we watched the "rushes" (more film talk meaning scenes shot the day before) and they were very dramatic! The Frisbee looked as if it were floating out off the screen and over the audience. The results pleased Lerner, but we still had another day to fill some spots.

Between takes, I threw some boomerang throws out over the water. I joked to a friend as I let one fly, "Hey, P.J., watch. I bet Lerner will want me to do these throws on camera!"

"As a matter of fact..." he said, coming up behind me. He not only wanted the throw on camera, but right at the camera.

Every time I made a good arching throw, the camera man lost sight of it. It seemed that when the camera man followed it, I would make a bad throw until finally, I threw one he followed perfectly. It actually landed right on top of the camera!

Although my part in the total film was small, it added quite a bit of zest. The film opens with a scene of P.J. and me playing Frisbee on the beach. Because of the 3-D effects, one of my throws to P.J. looks like it goes right over the audience.

After showing the two of us playing for a while, the camera slowly pans out into the sea for some exciting underwater shots, constantly taking advantage of the 3-D effects and then ends with a shot of a dolphin catching a Frisbee. Marineland even built a special million dollar theater to show it in.

I did manage to see the show once. "Excuse me, ladies and gentleman," a voice came over the speakers as the lights came on in the theater after the showing, "but we have in our audience the man who performed the Frisbee scenes—Peter Bloeme. Peter, take a bow." Well, if you insist, I thought, loving every minute of applause and the autographs. Show biz.

While films and TV shows are great for the resumé, television commercials are great for the pocketbook. They pay well and don't take much time. You're paid according to union rules based on how often you appear and how often the commercial is aired on television.

One of the best-known commercials I did was for Pepsi-Cola. I arrived for the shoot, hoping I might get a good-sized part, and it looked as though I would when the director told me he wanted me to drink some Pepsi-Cola on camera.

"Drink it without stopping. The entire bottle," I was told.

"Give me a break. How often do real people do that?," I thought.

"I hope you're thirsty," the director said as he walked away.

I wasn't.

There were two extras on the sidelines that were supposed to work with me on the shot. One was a girl who was supposed to hug me and pat me on the back like she was my girlfriend, while the other, a guy, was to wring a sponge out over my head to cool me off.

"And, action!," the director yelled.

I did my bit, running off to the sidelines. The girlfriend hugged me and the sponger started his bit.

"Yea, yea," she yelled. I was trying to drink this Pepsi-Cola all at once, she's thumping me on the back and the guy with the sponge, instead of wringing it over my head, hits me with it. This, in turn, caused my front teeth to knock into the bottle. Great. I'm gasping for breath, trying not to vomit and chipping my front teeth. All on film.

It took a while, but they finally had mercy on me and we ended with some good (safe) "refreshing" takes.

I obtained a good deal of satisfaction, though, as the final edit featured a move I call the windmill. I jump, spin in the air and catch the Frisbee between my legs with my hand in an upside-down position and land on my feet. Simply put, it's a move that resembles a flying-spinning-reverse-between-the-legs catch.

One of the most unusual requests I ever received was from a film-maker under contract with the United States Government. It seems that the U.S. Government, in the days before CNN, put together a film each month on American happenings, similar in format to *"Evening Magazine."* Each film consisted of different segments on business, art, sports—whatever. The filmmaker wanted to do the sports segment on Frisbee with Monika Lou, the 1976 Woman's World Champion and me. We got together for the shoot in San Francisco.

To the best of my knowledge, the film was designed for

1990 World Runner-up Bill Watters making his now famous Miller Lite pitch. Wizard, by the way was the "other" dog in one version of the commercial.

123

propaganda purposes, glorifying one "positive" side of the United States. I still don't know where, or how, it was ever used.

My exposure has not only been domestic, but I have also done many performances for international concerns. In the years since Alex Stein burst upon the scene at Dodger Stadium, the Ashley Whippet Celebrity Team has made quite an impact on the sporting world, including an appearance at Super Bowl XII. Because of this, we were invited by the NFL brass to an international event that made me feel as if we were a part of history—an NFL exhibition game in Berlin. Wizard and I joined Alex Stein with Ashley Whippet Jr. and Jeff Perry with Gilbert in performing before, between quarters and after the game at the American Bowl between the Los Angeles Rams and Kansas City Chiefs. After traveling to New York, Perry and I rendezvoused with Stein, who came in from Cleveland. From there we flew to Europe, transferred in Frankfurt and caught one final flight for Berlin.

I usually don't like transoceanic flights because they are long, tiring and smoky. But flying business class was different. Each time we boarded, we made sure the dogs had been put on the plane. We all were a little concerned about the long flight's effect on them because it was about 15 hours total for the dogs to spend in their kennels. Still, we would have been more concerned if they hadn't gotten on the correct flights. As it turned out when we claimed them in Berlin, they were all fine and eager to go.

We arrived on a Thursday morning, did the game Saturday and left Monday morning. Despite several required appearances during our visit, we managed to have a GREAT time. We went out each night and were able to experience German food and the night life.

The game took place Saturday, August 11, 1990 at 7:30 p.m. German time, at the Olympic Stadium (the home of the 1936 Olympic Games). Before the game there was a tremendous tailgate party on the grounds.

First International Ambassadog Tour, Jeff Perry & Gilbert; Alex Stein & Ashley Whippet Jr.; and Peter Bloeme & Wizard in Berlin, Germany.

Judging by the wild cheers, one would think that the crowd of 55,000 appreciated our performances even more than the game. During most of the play the spectators appeared more intent on doing the wave than paying attention to the game. This might have been because it was an early exhibition contest and there was not an abundance of action on the field as the August 20, 1990 issue of *Sports Illustrated* said:

"*On one of the fields the Frisbee dogs drew a bigger crowd than the subsequent practice game between the Dusseldorf Panthers and the Berlin Eagles [two local clubs].*"

Sunday was our last day, and we made the most of it by tearing down some of the Berlin Wall. Airport security people looked at us strangely at every stop on the flight back because of all the cement we had in our bags.

The flight back was faster and easier on the dogs since we went non-stop from Berlin to New York. We were able to take them out for a few minutes before checking them back in for their last leg of the trip.

I once heard a story about a world finalist who said that upon taking off in a plane, he heard his dog barking through the cabin floor. He banged on the floor to try to quiet him down. I thought it was a cute story but secretly wondered whether it was true until our flight from New York to Atlanta. Jeff Perry and I were in first class. The plane had started to push back from the terminal when it stopped to pick up some more baggage. It appeared as if more pets were loaded at the last second. We heard a bark, then a pause, then a bark then a pause, etc. Embarrassed, I recognized the bark as Wizard's. It took me a moment to figure out what had happened, but then it dawned on me that they must have put a cat next to Wizard's kennel. You may recall that Wizard thinks of cats as self-propelled Frisbees. So, naturally he barks to get them to move. Unfortunately, there was no place for either the cat or Wizard to go, so he just kept barking. To my relief, once we took off, the engines drowned out the sound. Perry, however, gave me grief the whole way home.

Of all the possible venues for showcasing Frisbee dogs, there is nothing better then a sporting event. We have done demonstrations during football, baseball, horse racing, soccer and many other games. Because of Wizard's skills, my favorite are basketball games.

There is nothing to compare with performing during the halftime at a NBA (National Basketball Association) game. I arrive early as the crowd starts to gather. The arena has a certain electricity to it. The artificial lights are ablaze and the music builds slowly with intensity. The building takes on life, the pace quickens, the crowd starts to buzz and the teams begin their warm-up. I watch all this from a corner, keenly aware of all that's going on around me: Children look for autographs, couples conversing, anticipation grows. Reality sets in as the world of advertising rears its not-so-subtle head and screams out the Budweiser message. It is announced that anyone caught throwing anything in the arena will be ejected. I glance down at Wizard.

It's funny, but a sellout crowd indoors in Charlotte, North Carolina, of over

24,000 Hornets fans can be more intimidating than the same crowd in the Dallas Cowboys football stadium. What makes it different and more exciting is that the floor is like a stage and the audience is close enough to see and be seen. The arena captures the cheers and boos and magnifies them 100%. To me, it's the perfect venue to display Wizard's intelligence, quickness and coordination.

The tension (for me) starts building when the first quarter ends. I start warming up and I check on Wizard from time-to-time to ensure he's resting comfortably in the locker room. With about five minutes left before halftime, I start getting nervous and put Wizard's custom made shoes on him (so he won't slip on the floor). Time begins to drag; the last few minutes seem to take forever. Finally, with one minute to go, Wizard and I are perched at the corner of the court. The buzzer goes off, my introduction begins and I tune everything out while Wizard goes nuts.

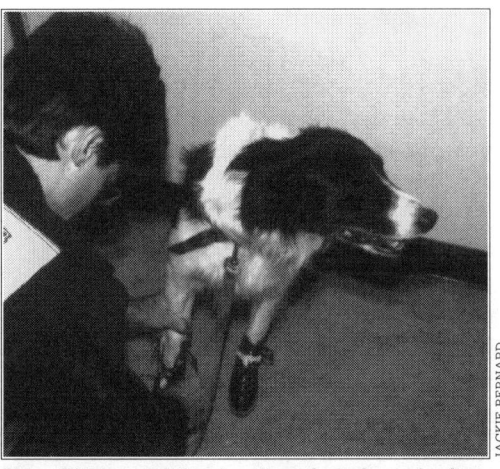

Peter Bloeme putting on the other champ's shoes for a NBA basketball halftime performance.

After one of our basketball shows, a sportswriter reported:

"How good was Jordan? Put it this way: Wizard the wonder dog, the world famous canine who entertained the fans at half with tremendous leaps for the Frisbee, was seen afterward taking notes from [Michael] Jordan as to the art of sky-walking."

Many projects I have been involved in had great potential, but for one reason or another they didn't come off. The music video *Top Dog* was one of them. One day I received a message on my answering machine from a television and film agent, named Robby Kass. He said he wanted to talk about two of his clients, David Wasson and Joe Karioth, who are screenwriters, songwriters, actors, musicians and singers. They were in the process of writing a song called *Top Dog* and he had mentioned my name to them because of Wizard. "Are you interested in speaking to them about doing a music video to go along with their song?" he asked. I said of course, so he gave me their telephone number. I called, not knowing what to expect. David sounded excited as I told him about Wizard and myself and I told him I would send him a videotape of us in action to give his partner and him a realistic image of what to expect.

They told me that once they viewed the tape, they went back and rewrote the song. They couldn't believe what Wizard and I could do. Plus, it was now easier for them to write because they had visuals they could work with.

A few weeks later, I met with Wasson, Karioth and their producer, Maggie Simon. Over dinner, we discussed different ideas about funding and locations for the video. By then they were fully aware of Wizard and my capabilities, while I had no way of knowing theirs. They invited me to the taping on Friday. When I arrived at the studio, I met the musicians—Bob the bass player, who had his Masters degree in music, Arnie a professional jazz drummer, Bobby the lead guitarist and Joie Gallo, the lead singer.

Top Dog sounded great. I had shown them some photos of Wizard in action and they were psyched. They ran through it a few times with Wasson making suggestions to Gallo on different techniques for the song—where to be clean, raspy, adjust pace, etc. It kept sounding better and better. Once the voice track was finalized, it was Bobby, the lead guitarist's, turn. Bobby, who looks like Jay Leno's twin, started by laying down one lead track, then another and finally a third, so that he was jamming with himself. He did a great job and sounded fantastic! I was amazed at how fast the whole thing came together. Everyone was a real professional.

By the end of the evening, the basic song was done. A song was written, recorded and produced for Wizard. I was excited! Unfortunately as many great and exciting projects sometimes do, this one hasn't yet gone anywhere. Here is *Top Dog* by David Wasson and Joe Karioth:

> "The streets are cold and filled with pain
> That's no place for a stranger
> You're just a face without a name
> Always looking at danger
> Never found the time to ask yourself why
> You learn the rules, then they change the game
> No one wants a beginner
> You've got the stuff to make your name
> You're the best. You're the winner
> Just want a chance to get up and fly
> You can be the top dog
> You can be the one to lead the pack
> You can be the top dog
> No time for sitting still or lookin' back
> (cause) you can be the top dog
> You can be the one to set the beat
> You can be the top dog
> You're the one to take the heat
> (You're running hard and breathin' fast)
> You're runnin' low and near the end
> Almost ready to give in
> You were reachin' out and you found a friend
> This is it. Now you're livin'
> All you need is just a little more time"

Afterword

With this book just a few weeks away from publication I decided there are a few last minute items to cover. Will this book GUARANTEE a world class dog or a world class trainer/thrower? Obviously not. After all, there are many factors involved in this sport. Are there other ways to accomplish the same goals than I have provided? Absolutely. This book contains a group of proven suggestions of methods that have worked for me and others in the sport. They are, by no means, the only ways. When you are dealing with different personalities, time, age and abilities of both dog and owner you have a myriad of options and possibilities. This makes it very difficult if you are trying to write a book on the subject but it also makes it fun, exciting and rewarding if you take the time and interest necessary to experiment and play with your canine partner. I hope this book has been helpful in guiding you in the right direction.

Almost everyone that I have worked with on this project has been extremely encouraging, cooperative and helpful about supplying their likenesses, photos, cartoons, suggestions and editorial input. Without that support this book would not have been possible.

Growth Of The Activity/Sport

In the last few years there has been a tremendous increase in interest from the commercial sector in the activity of canine Frisbee, from the entertainment and commercial industry. This has led to a number of television and print campaigns which have provided greater exposure and legitimacy for the activity/sport in a positive manner. As this continues, more dog and disc clubs will be founded, more people will get involved, and dogs all over will enjoy the benefits.

However, the positive elements of media exposure will continue only if those performers in the public eye temper their enthusiasm and keep their egos under control with the knowledge that if it weren't for the sport as we now know it, they would be on very different career paths. These people must continue to give back to the sport, and represent it in a respectful, beneficial, positive and professional manner at all times.

Future Of The Activity/Sport
One of the most positive directions the activity/sport is taking is in the development of dog and disc clubs. These clubs provide a not-for-profit forum for practitioners of the sport, in a "grass roots" manner. They provide an opportunity for shared insights with people who have the same interests, give demonstrations to entertain varied audiences including schools and charities and finally encourage the interest in others through exhibitions. Clubs not only promote competition, but friendship and sportsmanship, too. As valuable as clubs are, self-restraint should be practiced to avoid over-commercialization.

Concerns About The Activity/Sport
I am very pleased by the commercial interest and success the sport is enjoying. However, I am concerned that it will encourage people to enter the sport for the wrong reasons. Sadly, I have seen the human side of disc competition go in this direction.

There has always been a conscious effort by the founders of the sport of canine Frisbee to keep the value of prizes at a minimum. It was always felt that as the prizes grew in value, you would see a proportional decline in sportsmanlike behavior. The sport was developed for fun, comaraderie, good sportsmanship and responsible pet ownership as the key motivators.

Finally, competitors can't always look to the officials to police their behavior. If someone excessively complains about the judging, their score, etc., fellow competitors should make a point of letting him or her know that this is unacceptable, unhelpful and unproductive behavior. I have yet to see a dog owner complain about RECEIVING a higher score than he or she deserved. As mentioned earlier, judging is incredibly difficult and the officials do their best to be fair and impartial. Some days decisions will go your way and some days they won't. For example, there was a three-way tie in the South Central regional in 1990. The rules clearly stated the appropriate tie-breaker. The judges agonized over awarding third place to someone with a first place performance. The rules can work for or against anyone.

What The Sport Means To Me
I could wax philosophically on this one for quite some time so it's just as well that I'm almost out of space. Quite simply, I love the sport, challenge, dogs and people in it. I hope this book encourages new people to get involved in this activity in a positive and professional manner. Have fun!

Appendix

Recommended Reading

Dr. Pitcairn's Complete Guide to "Natural Health for Dogs and Cats"
by Richard H. Pitcairn, D.V.M, Ph. D, and Susan Hubbie Pitcairn
Rodale Press, Inc.
33 East Minor Street
Emmaus, PA 18049
Holistic views on canine care.

Athletes: Photographs 1960-1986
Edited by Ruth Silverman
Alfred A. Knopf
New York, NY
Coffee table book of photographs of athletes (includes one of Wizard).

Come 'N Get It Training Manual
By Irv Lander
P.O. Box 5862
Kalamazoo, MI 49003
For a free copy, send a self–addressed stamped envelope. Allow 8 weeks for shipment. Offer good only in the Continental U.S.A. Offer good while supplies last.

Dog Fancy Magazine
P.O. Box 53264
Boulder, CO 80322

Dog World Magazine
29 North Wacker Drive
Chicago, IL 60606

Dogs on Duty
by Catherine O'Neill
National Geographic Society
Washington, D.C.
Young adult book of working and performing dogs.

Frisbee Players Handbook
by Mark Danna & Dan Poynter
Parachuting Publications
P.O. Box 4232
Santa Barbara, CA 93103
The best book written on the myriad of throws, catches and events for the disc athlete.

Paul Loeb's Complete Book of Dog Training
by Paul Loeb
Prentice-Hall
Englewood Cliffs, NJ
Excellent book on dog training.

Super-Training Your Dog
by Jo and Paul Loeb
Prentice-Hall
Englewood Cliffs, NJ
This picks up where the last one left off.

Simon & Schuster's Guide To Dogs
Edited by Elizabeth Meriwether Schuler
Simon & Schuster, Inc.
1230 Avenue of the Americas
New York, New York 10020
"Over 320 breeds, each illustrated in full color, with a description of physical and personality characteristics, uses and care, such as gentle dog, watchdog or guard dog, needs clipping and many more…"

Traveling With Towser
Gaines TWT
P.O. Box 1007
Kankakee, Il 60902
This is a directory of hotels and motels across the country that accept guests traveling with dogs $1.25.

Equipment and Supplies
The following companies are great sources of Frisbees and related equipment, for the Frisbee dog enthusiast and will be happy to send you a catalog.

Disc Covering the World
P.O. Box 911
La Mirada, CA 90637
(714) 522-2202

The Wright Life
200 Linden
Ft. Collins, CO 80524
(303) 484-6932

Dog & Disc Clubs

Northeast
Ed Jakubowski
613 Norwich Road
Salem, CT 06415

North Central
Tom Wehrli
Chicago Dog and Disc Club
58130 Webster
Naperville, IL 60563

South
Jeff Perry
Greater Atlanta Dog and Disc Club
29 Golf Circle
Atlanta, GA 30309

South Central
Ron Ellis
Dallas/Ft. Worth Dog and Disc Club
7057 Pineberry Road.
Dallas, TX 75249

West
Mike Miller
1529 Golden Rose
Hacienda Heights, CA 91745

Northwest
Stan Sellers
Cascade Dog and Disc Club
1201 W Washington Ave, #40
Yakima, WA 98903

Contest Information

Inquiries regarding The Ashley Whippet Invitational Frisbee dog Championships should be addressed to:
Peter Bloeme, Deputy Director
Ashley Whippet Invitational
4060-D Peachtree Road, Suite 326
Atlanta, GA 30319
(404) 231-9240 (in GA)
(800) 786-9240 (outside GA)

Index

A
Advanced Frisbee Training, 73-86
    Back Flip, 83-84
    Butterfly, 85
    Cautions On Vaulting, 80-81
    Front Flip, 83-84
    Give/Drop, 77-78
    Multiple Disc Catches, 82-83
    Multiples, 81-82
    Over, 73-75
    Props, 85
    Take, 75-77
    Tapping, 84-85
    Vaulting, 78-81
Advanced Throws, 55-62
Afterword, 129-130
    Concerns About The Activity/Sport, 130
    Future Of The Activity/Sport, 130
    Growth Of The Activity/Sport, 129
    What The Sport Means To Me, 130
Air Major, 82, 106
Air Travel, 102-103
Allen, Frank, 93
Angel, 110
Appendix, 131-132
Arcuate Vane, 6
Ashley Whippet, 8-12, 15, 17, 19, 21, 87, 93, 118-119
Ashley Whippet, Jr., 9, 14,105, 124
Attitude, 98, 100

B
Back Flip, 83-84
Backhand Throw, 52-54
Ball(s), 23, 29, 67
Basic Frisbee Training, 63-72
    Catching, 69-71
    Frisbee Basics, 67-68
    Frisbee Familiarization, 66
    Jumping, 71
    Tracking, 66-67

    Warm-Ups, 68
    Weather Conditions, 65-66
    Workout Area, 63-65
Basic Throw And Catch, 88
Basic Training Techniques, 36-37
Barbo, Chris, 33, 87, 93
Bath(s), 29 , 32, 66
Baxter, 51, 99
Be Creative, 97-98
Beaches, 87-88
Belmond, 93
Bentley, 3
Berkeley Power Grip/Modified, 52-53
Bernard, Jackie, ii, 112
Blake, Reese, 77
Bloeme, Peter/Whirlin' Wizard, 15-25
Bone(s), 29, 31, 35, 45
Bouncin' Boo, 32, 38, 65, 82, 87, 89, 93, 114-115
Bowen, Tad, 86
Breit, Chris, 79, 92
Brookshire, Tom, 117
Brownell, Craig, 82-83
Butler, Rhett, 50
Butterfly Throw And Catch, 60, 85

C
Canine Frisbee History, 9-14
Carbo, 4
Carlos, Peter, 51, 90, 99
Carnation, 87
Catapult, 76, 78, 80, 121
Catching, 69-71
Carter, Amy, 10, 12, 69
Casey, 32, 58-59, 80, 93
Cautions On Vaulting, 80-81
Charity, 26, 81
Chest Vault, 62, 78, 80
Chew-toys, 29
China, 66
Chlorinated Water, 65
Choreography, 97, 98-99

133

Christian Science Monitor, 111, 116, 117
Clipper (nails), 34
Competitive Events, 88-91
Collar(s), 28-29, 63-64, 66, 68, 85
Collecting Discs, 107-110
Commands, 23, 35-37, 112
Common Injuries, 39
Communication, 36
Competition, 87-96
    Basic Throw And Catch, 88
    Competitive Events, 88-91
    Contest Promotion, 93
    Degree Of Difficulty, 90
    Execution, 90
    Freeflight, 89-91, 98
    Hall Of Famers, 93
    Judging, 92
    Leaping Ability, 90
    Local Competition, 91
    Mini-Distance, 88-89
    Regional And World Finals, 91
    Showmanship, 91
    World Champions, 93
Competition Tips, 97-100
    Be Creative, 97-98
    Choreography, 98-99
    Know The Rules, 97
    Practice All The events, 98
    Strategy, 99
    Working With The Media, 99-100
    Competition, 100
    Exhibition, 100
    General, 100
    Sponsor, 99-100
Concerns About The Activity/Sport, 130
Contest Promotion, 93
Cooling Your Dog, 65
Costume(s), 97-98
Cox, Bob, 87, 93
Crate(s), 101, 103

D

Degree Of Difficulty, 90
Delta, 52, 94
Delta Air Lines, 103
Dew-claws, 32
Dewormed, 29
Dink, 32, 87, 93
Disc Selection, 41-42
Discipline, 39
Dishwasher, 48
Distractions, 63
Dog And Disc Clubs, 129-130, 132
Driving, 102
Drop, 77-78

Duke, 75

E

Earle Palmer Brown, 93-94
Ears, 32
Ellis, Ron, 56-57, 64, 80-81, 85
Evans, Bob and Marilyn, 64
Exhibition(s), 99-100, 124-125, 130
Execution, 90

F

Farrow, Patrick Villers, 6
Fastbacks, 41-42
Fleas, 29, 32, 94
Food And Water, 105
Foreword, vii-viii
Frediani, Tony, 75
Freeflight, 89-91, 98
Freestyle, 18, 60
Frisbee Aerodynamics, 48-49
Frisbee Basics, 41-50, 67-68
    Frisbee Aerodynamics, 48-49
    Frisbee Care And Maintenance, 47-48
    Disc Selection, 41-42
    Gimmicks, 42-44
    Gumabone Frisbee Flexible Flying Disc, 44-47
Frisbee Care And Maintenance, 47-48
Frisbee Familiarization, 66
Front Flip, 83-84
Future Of The Activity/Sport, 130

G

Gabel, Jeff, 58-59, 80, 93
Gallo, Joie, 127
General Elements, 52
Gilbert, vi, 2, 32, 44-47, 64, 72, 75, 80, 93, 101, 105, 124
Gimmicks, 42-44
Give/Drop, 77-78
Gomes, Gary, 107, 114
Gorman, Ken, 87
Grip, 51-52
Grooming, 32
Growth Of The Activity/Sport, 129
Guidelines, 87-88, 90, 97
Gumabone Frisbee Flexible Flying Disc, 44-47
Guthrie, 39
Gyroscope, 48

H

Hall Of Famers, 87, 93
Hannah, 86
Hartshorne, Jeff, 50
Health, 28-32, 39, 64
History Of The Frisbee, 5-8

Holmes, Jendi, 21, 44, 96
Hoop, 76-77
Hoops, 71, 85
Hotels, 105
House-breaking, 37
How This Book Is Organized, 2
Hyper Hank, 11-13, 32, 69, 87, 93
Huender, Spencer, 34

I

Ice, 66, 105
Immunizations, 29
Injuries, 39
Introduction, 1-4
　How This Book Is Organized, 2
　Some Personal Thoughts, 2-3
Isis, 112

J

Jake, 32
Jordan, Michael, 87, 93, 126
Judging, 92
Jumping, 71

K

Karioth, Joe, 126-127
Kass, Robby, 126
Kato, 33, 87, 93
Kea, 36
Keep-Away, 67-69
Kelly, 107, 114
Kennels And Crates, 101-102, 124
Key Canine Considerations, 27-40
　Basic Training Techniques, 36-37
　Commands, 35-36
　Common Injuries, 39
　Discipline, 39
　Grooming, 32
　Health, 28-29
　Nails, 32-34
　Naming Your Dog, 31-32
　Nutrition, 30-31
　Obedience, 34-35
　Selecting A Dog, 27-28
　Teeth, 29-30
KFLA, 87
Kirkland, John, 17-19
Knerr, Rich, 6-7
Know The Rules, 97
Kona, 93

L

Lady Ashley, 12
Lander, Irv, viii, 10-13, 17, 93, 111, 115
Lander Cup, 13
Larson, Gary, 36
Leaping Ability, 90

Lehman, Bethe, 39
Leno, Jay, 127
Lerner, Murray, 121-122
Letterman, David, 10, 20, 117-121
Lite, No…Bud Light
Local Competition, 91
Loeb, Paul And Jo, 34
Lou, Monika, 118, 124

M

Maggie, Simon, 127
Maggy, 49, 56-57, 64-65, 80, 85
Mattie, 79, 92
McCammon, Lou, 62, 78, 80, 93
McIntire, Eldon, 11, 69, 87, 91, 93
Medford, Glen, 73-74
Melin, Spud, 6
Miller, Mike, 31, 76
Mini-Distance, 88-89
Morrison, Fred, 5-7
Multiple Disc Catches, 82-83
Multiples, 81-82
Mullen, Nancy, 111, 116
Mullennix, Cynthia, 23
Murphy, Bill, 114

N

Nails, 32-34
Naming Your Dog, 31-32
Neoprene Diving Vest, 73, 80
Nestle, 35
Nutrition, 30
Nylabone, 44-47

O

Obedience, 34-35
Octad, 17
Off-leash, 63, 68
Oui Magazine, 7
Over, 73-75
Overfeeding, 31
Overheated, 65, 105

P

Padgett, Cheryl, 1
Pads, 63, 66
Panting, 39, 65-66
Parvo, 29
Patent, 7, 18
Patience, 34, 37
Pawcolo, 28
Perry, Jeff, 44, 46, 72, 75, 80, 93, 101, 124
Peters, Sas, 32
Petersen, James R., 7
Pogson, Ken, 32
Practice All The Events, 98
Pro, 31, 76

135

Professional Appearances, 117-128
Props, 73, 85

R
Regional And World Finals, 91
Richie, 32
Rodriguez, Manny, 28
Roller, 54-55, 68-69, 83-84

S
Sam, 70
Sargent, Job, 15-16
Schatzie, 87
Schoech, Donna, 26, 81
Scooter, 62, 73, 78, 80, 87, 93
Scotland, 44, 96
Scully, Vin, 118
Sellers, Stan, 67
Showmanship, 91
Sidearm Throw, 57-58
Skip Throw, 55-57
Smith, Mike, 112
Some Personal Thoughts, 2-3
Stance, 51
Stein, Alex, 9-12, 14, 15, 19, 22, 31, 91, 93, 102, 111, 114-115, 118, 124
Strategy, 99
Steinbrenner, George, 120
Spin, 51
Sponsor, 99-100
Stance, 51
Sullivan, Paul, 113
Suzuki, Gary, 70

T
Take, 75-77
Talese, Gay, 5
Tap-Catch, 84
Tapping/Tipping, 60-61, 84-85
Tara, 43, 77
Tasha, 34
Taylor, Larry, 110
Teeth, 29-30
Teething, 29, 66
Tenite, 6
The Flight Explained, 103-105
Throwing, 51-62
 Advanced Throws, 55-62
 Backhand, 52-54
 General Elements, 52
 Grip, 51
 Roller, 54
 Sidearm, 57-58
 Skip, 55-57
 Spin, 51
 Stance, 51

Tapping/Tipping, 60-61
Two-Handed, 58-60
Upside-Down, 55
Upside-Down Slider, 54-55
Tipping, 60, 84
Tracking, 66-67
Travel, 101-106
 Air Travel, 102-103
 Food And Water, 105
 Hotels, 105
 Kennels And Crates, 101-102
 The Flight Explained, 103-105
TRC, 17
Treats, 31, 36-37
Tribune, Chicago, 113
Two-Handed Throw, 58-60

U
Ultimate, 19-20, 24
Upside-Down Throw, 55
Upside-Down Slider Throw, 54-55

V
Van, Tee Phil, v, 37, 48, 63, 68, 98
Vaulting, 78-81
Videotape, 97

W
Wakefield, Don, 4
Warm-Ups, 68
Wasson, David, 126-127
Watters, Bill, 82, 90, 106, 123
Weather Conditions, 65-66
Wehrli, Tom, 52, 94, 131-132
Westheimer, Ruth, 120
What The Sport Means To Me, 130
Whirlin' Wizard, 20-25
Whistle Disc, 42-44
Willett, Steve, 93, 115
Williams, Valdo, 16-17
Wizard's Competitive Experience, 111-116
Wood, Mark, 6, 40, 73, 80-81, 97
Working With The Media, 99-100
Workout Area, 63-65
World Champions, 93

Z
Zach, 6, 32, 40, 71, 97
Zulu, 67